Branches & Byways
Kent

'H'-class 0-4-4T No 31500 with a pull-push set of ex-SECR bogie stock at Goudhurst, awaiting departure to Paddock Wood with a train from Hawkhurst in the summer of 1960. *R. K. Blencowe collection*

Branches & Byways
Kent

John Scott-Morgan

OPC

An imprint of
Ian Allan Publishing

CONTENTS

Introduction	5
The Kent & East Sussex Railway	8
The East Kent Railway	22
The Sheppey Light Railway	34
The Hawkhurst Branch	42
The Port Victoria & All Hallows Branch	52
The New Romney and Dungeness Branches	62
The Canterbury & Whitstable Railway	74
The Folkestone Harbour Branch	82
The Hythe & Sandgate Branch	88
The Gravesend West Branch	94
The Elham Valley Railway	100
The Chatham Central Branch	104
The Westerham Branch	106
Index of Locations Illustrated	112

Acknowledgements

I am grateful to the following photographers — some of whom, sadly, are no longer with us — whose images have been used in this book: R. Blencowe, R. C. Riley, R. M. Casserley, R. J. Buckley, Roger Carpenter, C. Hamilton Ellis, J. H. L. Adams, H. C. Casserley, R. E. Tustin, J. H. Aston, R. F. Roberts, A. W. V. Mace, P. J. Garland, J. Grant, E. A. Woollard, G. W. Batchelor, E. E. Smith, H. F. Wheeler, E. E. Banks, P. Ransomm-Wallis, J. W. Sparrowe, P. Winding, M. D. England, F. J. Agar, H. P. Rut, K. W. Wightman, D. Cross, W. A. Camwell, E. Carpenter, S. W. Baker, J. C. Flemons, M. J. Fair, P. A. Harding, H. J. P. Rutherford, W. F. Wheeler and E. Course; thanks are due also to the Lens of Sutton collection and to the Colonel Stephens Museum at Tenterden.

Finally I should like to thank Kirk Martin for typing the manuscript for this book.

Dedication

For John Odell, modeller, Southern enthusiast and friend.

Front cover: 'C'-class 0-6-0 No 31588 arrives at Cranbrook on 10 June 1961 with a special train of Maunsell corridor stock bound for Hawkhurst. *R. C. Riley*

Back cover (upper): A tranquil scene at Hawkhurst on 20 May 1961, three weeks before closure of the branch, as 'H'-class 0-4-4T No 31543 and a pull-push set await departure from a near-deserted platform. *R. C. Riley*

Back cover (lower): 'H'-class 0-4-4T No 31530 awaits departure from Westerham with a push-pull train for Dunton Green on 8 October 1961. *Rodney Lissenden*

Title page: Class A1X 'Terrier' No 32655 heads south to Rolvenden from Tenterden Town station on 27 July 1953 after shunting the goods yard, while the porter signalman walks up the platform to attend to some recently arrived luggage. *R. C. Riley*

First published 2008

ISBN 978 0 86093 616 9

© Ian Allan Publishing Ltd 2008

Published by Oxford Publishing Co

an imprint of Ian Allan Publishing Ltd, Hersham, Surrey, KT12 4RG
Printed in England by Ian Allan Printing Ltd, Hersham, Surrey, KT12 4RG

Code: 0810/B

Visit the Ian Allan Publishing website at www.ianallanpublishing.com

INTRODUCTION

An 'H'-class tank and its pull-push train eases to a stand still at Goudhurst on its journey to Hawkhurst. The locomotive crew chat to the stationmaster as a porter humps a trolley of parcels from the brake van and wheels it up the platform to the parcels room. In a short while the signalman pulls off the upper-quadrant signal, the guard blows a whistle, and the 0-4-4T is off on its journey through the hop fields and Kent countryside. Such was the essence of a way of life, now long gone, which linked the local branch-line railway to the village community, pacing the hours of each day and providing the local people with a link with the hustle and bustle of the outside world.

The rural branch lines of Kent evolved from the 1830s through to the 1900s to provide this important connection for rural people and goods and afforded new and improved outlets and markets for produce from this lush and fertile corner of England. A major part of the drive and impetus for constructing these vital arteries of commerce came from the local people themselves, who raised the finance to build these sometimes risky undertakings.

Many of the lines promoted from the 1860s to the 1890s were the result of bitter rivalry between the South Eastern Railway and the London, Chatham & Dover Railway. This in turn was the result of a bitter feud between two powerful men — Sir Edward Watkin, Chairman of the South Eastern Railway, and James Staats-Forbes, Chairman of the London, Chatham & Dover Railway — which led to some development projects which were a waste of time and money.

The rivalry came to an end in 1899 with the formation of the South Eastern & Chatham Joint Managing Committee, which was in effect a form of amalgamation of the two companies. This arrangement continued until 1922, when both companies negotiated an agreement to become part of the newly formed Southern Railway, with effect from 1 January 1923.

The branch lines covered in this book were in the main promoted as small concerns by local people and were operated on their behalf by either the SER or the LCDR. In many cases the original railway would within a few years of opening be taken over by the larger operating company, and in the main this made good business and economic sense.

After the formation in 1899 of the SECR Joint Committee the railways of Kent settled down to a peaceful existence which continued until the late 1950s and early 1960s, when in the main closures took place under British Railways management. In addition to the branch lines built with the backing of the main-line companies there were two substantial railways built under the direction of Lt Col Holman Fred Stephens, these being the Kent & East Sussex Railway and the East Kent Railway. Both of these extensive lines were constructed between 1899 and 1925.

The Kent & East Sussex Railway, opened in 1900 as the Rother Valley Railway, operated a line from Robertsbridge, in East Sussex, to Headcorn via the market town of Tenterden. The East Kent Railway operated a line with two branches, which served the Kent Coalfield near Dover, the main line of which ran from Shepherdswell to Wingham Canterbury Road with a branch to Richborough Harbour from a junction at Eastry. The East Kent Railway's main source of traffic was coal from Tilmanstone Colliery, which remained open until the 1980s.

Right: British Railways poster from the 1950s. *BR*

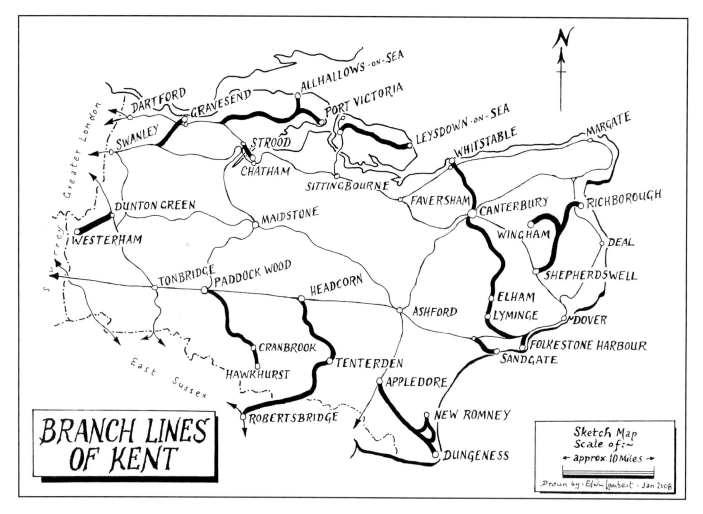

BRANCH LINES OF KENT

Sketch Map
Scale of:~
← approx. 10 Miles →

Drawn by · Edwin Lambert · Jan 2008

The branch lines and rural byways of Kent had about them a magic that has been sadly lost in a 21st-century world of tedious standardisation. Yet even today the county's lines and their operation, ranging from the density of London's southeastern suburbs to the remoteness of Romney Marsh, represent an amazing contrast of urban and rural branch networks.

Like most branch lines, those in Kent started life as neat additions to the main-line network but went into decline after World War 1, as the decades went past and as a result of road competition, which ended in the closure of most in the early 1960s during the time of the Kent Coast electrification. The county's branch network was predominantly steam-worked, only a few lines ever seeing diesel operation. Rumours in the late 1950s and early 1960s that certain branches were to be electrified

turned out to be just that, as in every case the line concerned eventually closed. Indeed, such is the extent of obliteration that, in most cases, anyone searching for the remains of the lines featured in this book will be lucky to find a mound in a field or an odd section of fence, the only real exceptions being a section of the Kent & East Sussex Railway and a small fragment of the East Kent Railway, which are preserved. Thus, in the space of a century and a half, history has turned full circle, and the intervening period is an era we can experience only in our memories and our dreams.

John Scott-Morgan
Woking
July 2008

Left: 'H'-class 0-4-4T No 31533 at Hawkhurst on a summer's afternoon in July 1959, having just arrived with a train from Paddock Wood. This picture shows to good effect the corrugated-iron station building. *Roger Carpenter*

Above: 'H'-class 0-4-4T No 31553 simmers in the empty platform at Allhallows on Sea in the summer of 1955 with a train for Gravesend Central. The driver has yet to set up the headcode and prepare the locomotive for departure. *R. K. Blencowe collection*

Above right and right: The fate of most of the branch lines featured in this volume — derelict station building, weed-strewn track and a demolition gang ripping out the very heart of the line. These photographs record the scene at Goudhurst, on the Hawkhurst branch, on 25 March 1964. *R. C. Riley*

THE KENT & EAST SUSSEX RAILWAY

Opened on 2 April 1900, the Rother Valley Railway was one of the first light railways to be built in Britain under the terms of the Light Railways Act 1896. Part of the Colonel Stephens group of lines, it ran originally from Robertsbridge, in East Sussex, to a location south of Tenterden, being connected to the Kent town by a horse-bus service.

On 16 March 1903 the line was extended to a new Tenterden Town station, the old terminus being renamed Rolvenden, while on 1 June 1904 the railway itself was renamed as the Kent & East Sussex Railway. In conjunction with the South Eastern & Chatham Railway a further extension was built as far as Headcorn, this section opening to traffic on 15 May 1905. Parliamentary assent had also been given for a link between Headcorn and Maidstone, but, like other proposed extensions, to Pevensey, Rye and Cranbrook, this ultimately came to nought.

In its early days the railway had been a very smart affair, locomotives being painted Oxford blue in a style not unlike that of the Great Eastern Railway, while carriage stock was light brown.

The latter comprised six four-wheelers supplied by Hurst Nelson in 1900, which were rebuilt on bogie frames in 1904. They were joined in 1905 by a set of three more bogie vehicles built by R. Y. Pickering for the Headcorn extension.

The locomotive fleet consisted of a collection of new and second-hand machines. Two Hawthorn Leslie 2-4-0Ts, No 1 *Tenterden* and No 2 *Northiam*, ready in time for the opening in 1900, were joined in 1901 by No 3 *Bodiam*, a 'Terrier' 0-6-0T acquired from the London, Brighton & South Coast Railway, and another Hawthorn Leslie locomotive, 0-8-0T No 4 *Hecate*, built in 1904 for the proposed Maidstone extension. A further Brighton 'Terrier', No 5 *Rolvenden*, was acquired in 1906.

Below: A general view of the Kent & East Sussex bay platform and the goods yard at Robertsbridge. The photograph, taken in the direction of Hastings, dates from 27 July 1955, 18 months after the cessation of passenger services. *R. M. Casserley collection*

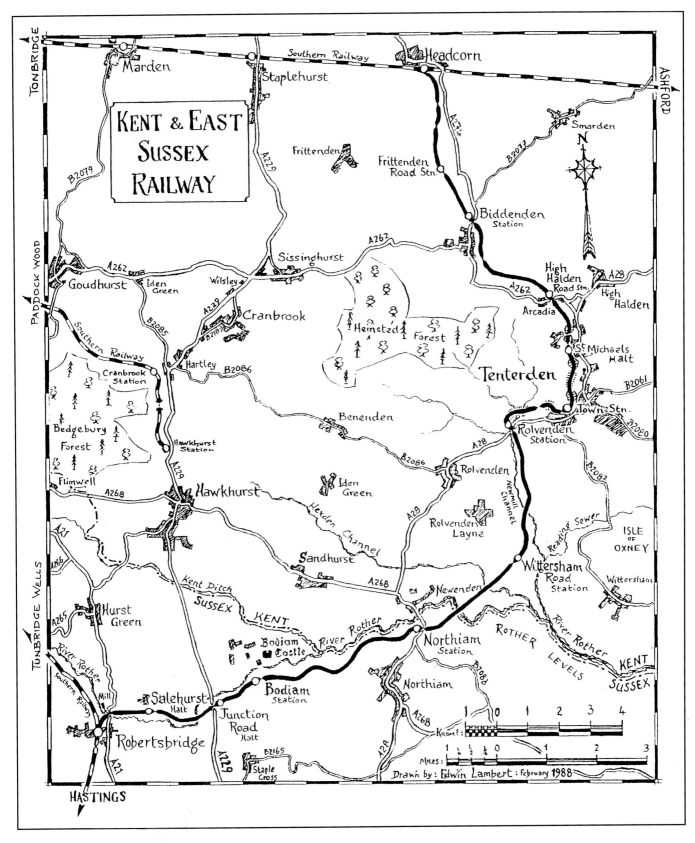

KENT & EAST SUSSEX RAILWAY

Drawn by: Edwin Lambert: February 1988

In 1906 the railway acquired an R. Y. Pickering four-wheeled steam railcar, which became No 6; later renumbered 16 in the carriage register, this machine was not a great success, spending most of its life on the dump at Rolvenden. Locomotive No 7 *Rother*, an 'Ilfracombe' 0-6-0 goods locomotive acquired in 1910 from the London & South Western Railway, was followed in 1914 by No 8 *Hesperus*, an ex-Great Western Railway 0-6-0ST, and another ex-LSWR 'Ilfracombe', No 9 *Juno*.

The railway's station buildings were generally of simple construction, those on the original Rother Valley section being of corrugated iron and those on the Headcorn extension of timber, although Tenterden Town station was brick-built. There were two major bridges on the Rother Valley section, one near Junction Road Halt and a second over the River Rother, between Northiam and Wittersham Road stations. There was only one tunnel, near Tenterden St Michael's Halt.

Although the company did well in its early years, things started to take a turn for the worse after World War 1, when the ready availability of motor-lorry chassis and complete army-surplus vehicles encouraged large numbers of ex-servicemen to set themselves up in business as bus operators and/or road hauliers. By the mid-1920s the railway was starting to feel the pinch, and economy measures were implemented, among them the introduction of railbus sets. Three such sets — two Fords and a Shefflex — ran on the line from the early 1920s until the mid-1930s but proved a mixed blessing, as they were not the most comfortable vehicles in which to ride and often smelled strongly of petrol.

In the inter-war years the railway settled down to a peaceful existence as a rural byway, becoming much loved by the public and enthusiasts alike. The Colonel died in 1931 and was succeeded as Manager by W. H. Austen, who would keep the railway going until nationalisation on 1 January 1948.

In 1932 locomotive No 4 *Hecate* was exchanged with the Southern Railway for a second-hand 0-6-0ST, ex-London & South Western Railway No E0334, and two spare boilers. By the mid-1930s most of the original fleet of steam locomotives had become worn out, and from 1936 until nationalisation the company had to hire locomotives from the Southern Railway, these taking the form of 'P'-class 0-6-0 tanks, Class A1X 'Terriers', 'O1'-class 0-6-0s and, for a time, '0395' 0-6-0s. The company also had a mixed collection of four-wheel, six-wheel and bogie rolling stock that was purchased second-hand over the years.

During World War 2 the War Department stationed rail-mounted guns at Rolvenden as part of the anti-invasion precautions. The line was also used as an alternative route for military traffic and during the build-up to D-Day formed part of Pipe Line PLUTO.

After the war improvements were made to the track and station lighting at various points along the line, and after British Railways took over in 1948 more improvements were made, including re-laying most of the track with materials from the Elham Valley line. But this did not stem the losses, which resulted in the railway's closure to passengers on 2 January 1954; at the same time all goods and passenger services north of Tenterden Town were withdrawn. Thereafter the service was confined to goods trains — plus occasional hop-pickers' and enthusiasts' specials — between Robertsbridge and Tenterden Town, which continued until 11 June 1961.

Shortly after closure a preservation society was formed which has succeeded in preserving and reopening the line south of Tenterden as far as Bodiam and hopes in due course to extend its operations thence to Robertsbridge.

Left: On 3 July 1953 Class A1X 'Terrier' No 32655 (nowadays preserved on the Bluebell Railway) simmers at the bay platform at Robertsbridge with a single LSWR bogie Brake First/Third carriage forming the 8.15am to Tenterden Town. *R. J. Buckley*

Left: KESR No 3, a Class A1 'Terrier' 0-6-0T (formerly LBSCR No 70 *Poplar*), arrives at Robertsbridge with a single ex-LSWR Panter bogie non-corridor Brake Third forming a train from Tenterden Town *c* July 1936. Note the large brick water tower and double SECR water crane in the middle background and the single version on the platform. *R. M. Casserley collection*

Above: Northbridge Street level crossing near Hodsons Mill, which had the only industrial siding on the KESR. This photograph, taken *c*1936 in the direction of Tenterden Town, shows the original RVR double home signal and the wind pump for the water tower. *Roger Carpenter collection*

Above right: Salehurst Halt *c*1952, viewed in the direction of Robertsbridge Junction. This is a good example of the basic structures found on most of the Colonel's lines, lacking a shelter and being located a fair distance from the village it purported to serve. However, there is a weather-beaten bench on which to sit, so passengers had to be thankful for small mercies. *Pamlin Prints*

Right: The second Junction Road Halt, constructed from concrete parts in 1946 and viewed here in June 1953 in the direction of Tenterden Town. This structure replaced a timber-and-ash platform similar to that at Salehurst Halt. *Author's collection*

Right: KESR 0-6-0ST No 4 (ex SR No E0334) at Bodiam *c*1936 with a train for Robertsbridge. The group of people in front of the locomotive are hop-pickers, probably on their way to Robertsbridge Junction to do some shopping. *C. Hamilton Ellis*

Left: Photograph of Bodiam station taken *c*1938 in the direction of Tenterden Town and showing the goods yard full of coal wagons; note also the hop fields in the background, with the oasthouses of the Guinness's hop farm on the far right. This station was one of the original Rother Valley structures built of corrugated iron and timber. *Author's collection*

Below left: Northiam station *circa* July 1953, viewed in the direction of Tenterden Town. The station building was similar to that at Bodiam and built of the same materials, but the platform was slightly longer and in 1946 had electric platform lighting installed. Note that the far end of the platform is raised for milk-churns, this being another modification of 1946. *Author's collection*

Below: The mid-morning mixed train for Tenterden Town simmers in the platform at Northiam while the station agent unloads an LMS van next to the ex-LSWR Panter bogie Brake Third in the summer of 1936. Class A1 'Terrier' 0-6-0T No 3 had only recently returned to service after an extensive rebuild incorporating parts donated by sister No 5 *Rolvenden* and fittings from another 'Terrier' on the Shropshire & Montgomeryshire Light Railway. *C. Hamilton Ellis*

Right: Wittersham Road station from the road *c*1930. This is a good view of the station building, which was at a right-angle to the platform and lacked an awning. Note that the station still retained its gates, unlike the majority of stations on the line, which had these removed by the Colonel as a cost-cutting exercise but to the detriment of safety. *Author's collection*

Below: The double-arm signal at Wittersham Road *c*1936, with the station building in the background. *C. Hamilton Ellis*

Above: Rolvenden station on 5 May 1935, viewed in the direction of Tenterden Town. This was the original Tenterden station, opened 2 April 1900, with a horse-bus connection to Tenterden High Street. This photograph shows an interesting collection of corrugated-iron buildings, including the printer's hut and the lamp room (far right). On the right, behind the station nameboard, stands the line's ex-Midland Railway six-wheel breakdown crane. *J. H. L. Adams*

Left: Rolvenden station building viewed in the direction of Robertsbridge Junction on 3 July 1953, with Class A1X 'Terrier' No 32655 standing by the water column. This photograph shows clearly the milk-churn platform; note also the Coronation poster on the station notice board. *R. J. Buckley*

Above: The second Ford railbus set at the station platform at Rolvenden *c*1935, with a group of station staff and passengers posing for the photographer.
Author's collection

Right: Over the hills and far away … The tranquillity of Rolvenden is broken briefly on 19 August 1933 by the departure of the 11.15am passenger train to Headcorn Junction, consisting of a single ex-LSWR bogie Brake Third with 0-6-0ST No 4 at its head, which has just left the station and is heading for Tenterden Bank. Arcadia at its finest, this view more than any other in this volume sums up the British light railway.
H. C. Casserley

Above left: Class A1X 'Terrier' No 2678, on hire from the Southern Railway, on shed at Rolvenden *c*1946. The wagon behind the locomotive is of interest, being one of four open wagons, all of LBSCR origin, purchased from the SR in the late 1940s to replace the initial stock of Rother Valley open wagons.
Lens of Sutton collection

Left: Having replaced ex-LSWR Adams 0-6-0 No 3440, 'Terrier' No 3 prepares to set off from Rolvenden on 26 April 1947 with the 8.50am for Robertsbridge Junction. This picture shows to good effect the two-road locomotive shed.
H. C. Casserley

Right: Cresting the bank at Tenterden Town station in June 1953 is Class A1X 'Terrier' No 32655 with a single ex-LSWR bogie corridor First/Third carriage forming a train from Robertsbridge Junction. This is a good view of the three-arm signal.
Author's collection

Above: A general view of the goods yard at Tenterden Town from the Headcorn end (*i.e.* towards Robertsbridge Junction), with the coal yard on the left and the Ministry of Food depot sidings on the right. The centre roads led to the station, while the corrugated-iron building on the far right housed the yard ground-frame. *Pamlin Prints / R. M. Casserley collection*

Above left: 'O1' 0-6-0 goods No 1434 leaves Tenterden Town with a train for Robertsbridge Junction in the winter of 1949. *R. M. Casserley collection*

Left: View of Tenterden Town station in the summer of 1948, showing the station platforms and the Ministry of Food store at the rear of the island platform on the western side of the station. A train for Headcorn Junction waits at the main platform. *Lens of Sutton collection*

Above right: Tenterden St Michaels Halt, with its basic timber platform lacking any sort of shelter. This was the view towards Tenterden Town on 21 November 1953, a mere six weeks before closure. *Pamlin Prints / R. M. Casserley collection*

Right: Through the sunlight and shadows of a summer's day 'O1'-class 0-6-0 No 31048 and its single ex-LSWR corridor Brake First/Third forming the 11.32am train to Headcorn Junction head sedately through St Michael's Tunnel and onward to High Halden Road on 17 May 1952. *Pamlin Prints / R. M. Casserley collection*

17

Above: 'O1' No 31064 departs High Halden Road station with a train for Tenterden Town in the summer of 1952. Note that, as in the previous picture, the train lacks any sort of headcode. *Author's collection*

Left: High Halden Road on 21 November 1953. The photograph, taken in the direction of Headcorn Junction, shows the station's timber building and the double-arm home signal, similar to that at Wittersham Road. *Pamlin Prints / R. M. Casserley collection*

Left: A very early photograph of Biddenden station, taken in the direction of Tenterden Town shortly after completion of the Headcorn extension (opened 15 May 1905). The locomotive is one of the original Hawthorne 2-4-0Ts (No 1 *Tenterden* or No 2 *Northiam*), while the train consists of two ex-LSWR six-wheel carriages sandwiched between a pair of ex-North London Railway brake vans. Awaiting its arrival are the station agent and a young man wearing a straw boater. Just discernible on the far right, near the points, is a velocipede, used for inspecting the line. *Author's collection*

Above: Biddenden station viewed in the direction of Tenterden Town on 30 August 1938, looking clean and well-kempt. This was one of three KESR stations that had passing-loops and two platforms, the others being Northiam and Tenterden Town, but the loop at Biddenden was the only one to remain in use until the end. The building on the far right was the station agent's bungalow.
Roger Carpenter

Right: 'O1' 0-6-0 No 31064 approaching Biddenden station *c*1953 with a single ex-LSWR bogie corridor First/Third carriage forming a train from Headcorn Junction to Tenterden Town. *Author's collection*

Left: The essence of a rural byway miles from the village it served: Frittenden Road station on 30 August 1938, with the double-arm home signal used by passengers to stop trains by request. This was the view towards Headcorn Junction. *Roger Carpenter*

Below: A later view of Frittenden Road, its deep slumber momentarily interrupted by the passing of 'O1'-class 0-6-0 No 31065 (nowadays preserved on the Bluebell Railway) with the Headcorn Junction–Tenterden Town service on 23 August 1952. *Pamlin Prints / R. M. Casserley collection*

Right: The original Headcorn Junction station *c*1910, with a train of three ex-LSWR six-wheel carriages at the straight, brick-built platform. Erected originally at Tenterden Town, the station building had been dismantled at that location and transported to Headcorn as a set of corrugated-iron parts. *Author's collection*

Above: The later, rebuilt Headcorn Junction station, with its concrete curved platform and modified track layout, photographed on 10 April 1939. Hired SR Class A1X 'Terrier' 0-6-0T No 2655, which seems to have spent a lot of its time on the Kent & East Sussex Railway, waits to depart with a single ex-LSWR non-corridor Brake Third. Note that the locomotive still has condensing pipes fitted. *R. E. Tustin*

Below: On hire to the KESR in the summer of 1948, Class A1X 'Terrier' 0-6-0T No 2640 shunts the exchange sidings that led from Headcorn Junction station to the gate that had defined the boundary between SR and KESR property. At the beginning of 1948 the KESR had ceased to exist, but until June the line (along with the other railways that had formed Col Stephens' empire) was managed for British Railways by W. H. Austen from the head office at 23 Salford Terrace, Tonbridge. *Lens of Sutton collection*

THE EAST KENT RAILWAY

One of the positive aspects of the first Channel Tunnel project in the 1880s was the discovery of coal in East Kent. Sir Edward Watkin's tunnel might not have been built, but as a result of the discovery of seams of coal there was hope of some kind of compensation for all the good money that had been seemingly thrown after bad.

In the late 1890s and early 1900s a group of businessmen came together to form a syndicate to sink the collieries in order to exploit this new mineral wealth. Some of the finances for this came from Britain, but there were also significant contributions from France and elsewhere overseas.

In the event 40 bores were sunk in and around the district between Dover and Richborough to ascertain the size of the coalfield. As a result of this activity four collieries were opened, at Tilmanstone, Chislet, Snowdown and Betteshanger, which remained in operation until the 1980s, when they were closed by the National Coal Board. Coal mines were also sunk at Guilford, Hammill and Wingham, but these workings never went into production.

The history of the syndicate and its many proposed lines is a complicated one. Suffice it to say that between 1910 and 1928 there were 40 applications for light-railway orders made for the main route and extensions to the railways, which made up the East Kent system.

As with the Kent & East Sussex Railway, the company's civil engineer was Lt Col Holman Fred Stephens, who directed developments from his office at 23 Salford Terrace, Tonbridge. The East Kent was a very different railway from the Kent & East Sussex in that it was constructed to a heavier profile, utilising on the southern portion some quite heavy steel bridges and heavyweight flat-bottom and second-hand bull-head rail.

The railway was designed to connect all the aforementioned collieries with the South Eastern & Chatham main line at Shepherdswell, on the Canterbury–Dover main line, and with the Dover–Ramsgate main line at Richborough, where during the Great War a military port was established. A further line was built from a junction at Eastry to Wingham (Canterbury Road), a station in the middle of nowhere on the way to Canterbury. There were originally plans to link this line with the main line at Brakesbourne, but this project, like many others to do with the EKR, came to nothing.

The first stage of the network opened in 1911 on a temporary line from Shepherdswell to Tilmanstone Colliery, which ran around Golgotha Hill, while a tunnel was being dug through the hill. A company called the East Kent Contract & Financial Co Ltd had been set up to build the railway in 1911. By October 1912 the line had reached Eastry and the tunnel at Golgotha Hill, which was built to double-track size and had now been completed. This meant that the temporary line could be dismantled.

After reaching Eastry the line divided at a junction, the branch north going to Richborough Port and the western branch going to Wingham (Canterbury Road). By October 1912 the company had built the branch to Guilford Colliery from Eythorne. The section of line from Eastry to Wingham Colliery, along with a short branch to Hammill Colliery, was constructed the same year. The short section from Wingham Colliery to Wingham Town was not completed until 1920.

The first signs of over-optimism had appeared by 1914, by which time both Wingham and Hammill collieries had already closed.

Left: In many respects the East Kent Railway was for those with a keen sense of adventure — it was better to travel than to arrive at places like Wingham Canterbury Road or Sandwich Road. Purchasing a ticket from someone in a building resembling a garden shed, as here at Shepherdswell, must have been a good start. The carriages await on an August morning in 1937.
Roger Carpenter

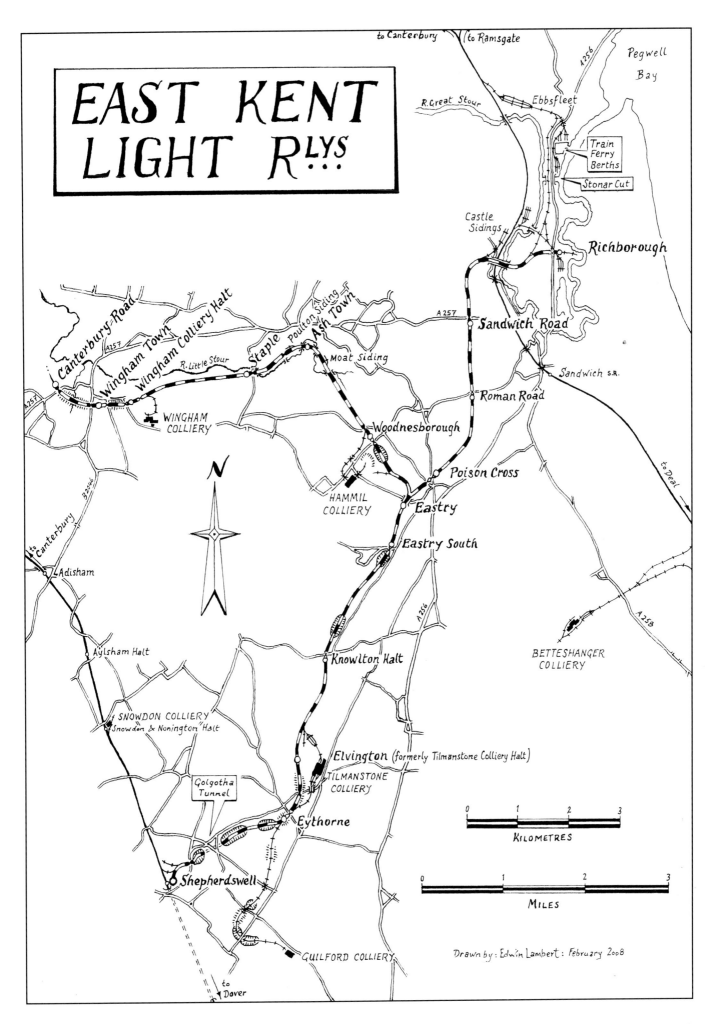

EAST KENT LIGHT R^{LYS}

to Canterbury to Ramsgate Pegwell Bay

R. Great Stour Ebbsfleet

Train Ferry Berths

Stonar Cut

Castle Sidings

Richborough

Canterbury Road Wingham Town Wingham Colliery Halt Poulton Siding Staple Ash Town

A 257 Sandwich Road

R. Little Stour Moat Siding

Sandwich S.R.

WINGHAM COLLIERY

Roman Road

Woodnesborough

HAMMIL COLLIERY

Poison Cross

to Canterbury

Eastry

Adisham

Eastry South

Aylsham Halt

to Deal

BETTESHANGER COLLIERY

A 256

Knowlton Halt

SNOWDON COLLIERY Snowdon & Nonington Halt

Elvington (formerly Tilmanstone Colliery Halt)

Golgotha Tunnel

TILMANSTONE COLLIERY

Eythorne

Shepherdswell

GUILFORD COLLIERY

to Dover

0 1 2 3 KILOMETRES

0 1 2 3 MILES

Drawn by: Edwin Lambert: February 2008

23

In fact the colliery at Guilford never opened to production, even though the pithead buildings had been constructed. As far as the East Kent Railway was concerned the only colliery to show any potential was Tilmanstone, at the Shepherdswell end of the line. Although it was intended that the other collieries that had been sunk and later closed or mothballed were to be opened at some point in the future, this never happened.

In 1916 the railway obtained permission to operate a passenger service from Sheperdswell to Wingham, and in the same year the War Department decided to develop Richborough as a major military port. Although the EKR was building a line north from Eastry it did not reach Richborough until 1928, by which time the port was no longer an important source of potential revenue for the railway. The main cause of this long period of development for such a short section of line was the need to build a series of bridges across the road to Richborough Castle and the River Stour and also the main Dover–Ramsgate line at that point after a series of rather makeshift bridges had been built to take the line to Richborough Port.

The EKR was not allowed to run passenger trains between Sandwich Road and Richborough Port Halt, as the bridge was not passed for passenger trains. A passenger service was operated from Eastry to Sandwich Road from August 1925, but this continued only until 31 October 1928, ceasing before the EKR had opened its line to Richborough Port, in 1929. This situation was due largely to the Government's selling the port to Dorman Long, which was less than enthusiastic about doing business with the railway company, and as a result Richborough Port never saw passengers.

Like the Kent & East Sussex Railway, the EKR had plans to build extensions to Canterbury, Stodmarsh and Deal, but, again like those of the KESR, these came to nothing; apart from the Richborough line the only extension constructed was that from Wingham Town to Wingham Canterbury Road, 1½ miles away, as part of the project to build a connection to Canterbury. Wingham Canterbury Road was originally called simply Wingham and was typically Colonel Stephens in that it was a very long way from Canterbury and, as the line was never extended further, served nothing but a neighbouring field!

During World War 2 the Army operated rail-mounted guns on the section from Eastry to Sandwich Road station, which at that time was open only for goods traffic. This was part of the defence of southern England after the fall of France in 1940. After the war

Above: The locomotive shed at Shepherdswell in the late 1930s, with 'O'-class 0-6-0 No 6 on shed and Kerr Stuart 0-6-0T No 4 out of use awaiting a boiler wash-out. Alongside No 4 can be seen the chassis of No 2 *Walton Park* undergoing a rebuild, while in the foreground is the ex-Midland Railway six-wheel crane, complete with runner. *H. C. Casserley*

the line went through a period of improvement like that on the Kent & East Sussex Railway. The stations, which were more like garden sheds than conventional stations, were repainted, as were the fences and platform edges. The track was weeded, and some renewal took place.

In common with most of the Colonel Stephens lines that remained open, the East Kent Railway was nationalised on 1 January 1948. The passenger service was destined not to last long, the last train running on 1 November 1948. The Richborough branch closed on 27 October 1949, when its last goods train ran, followed by the Eastry–Canterbury Road goods service which closed on 25 July 1950, and finally the line north of Eythorne to Eastry closed on 1 March 1951. From then until final closure of the line from Sheperdswell to Tilmanstone Colliery, in April 1984, little changed on the remaining section of the East Kent Railway apart from dieselisation in the early 1960s and the use from the early 1970s of Class 73 electro-diesels.

Like most of the other Colonel Stephens railways, the EKR was over-stocked with locomotives and rolling stock. Its first locomotive was an ex-Great Western 0-6-0 saddle tank built by Fox Walker in 1875, which was used in the construction of the line and withdrawn in 1935. No 2 named *Walton Park,* was an 0-6-0ST built in 1908 by Hudswell Clarke and had formerly worked on the Weston, Clevedon & Portishead Railway; withdrawn in 1941, it was sold for further industrial service, being finally cut up in 1959. No 3 was an unrebuilt 'Ilfracombe' 0-6-0 goods locomotive built in 1880 by Beyer Peacock for the London & South Western Railway. It was acquired by the EKR in 1916 and was withdrawn in 1928.

No 4 was an ex-War Department 'Victory'-class 0-6-0T built by Kerr Stuart & Co in 1917; purchased in 1911 by Consolidated Kent Collieries, it was used at Tilmanstone Colliery, it lasted into British Railways days, being withdrawn in 1949. No 5, an ex-LSWR

Adams Radial 4-4-2T built in 1882, had had an interesting history, having been sold to the War Department during World War 1 prior to acquisition by the EKR in 1919. After being stored by the railway for some years it was sold in 1946 to the Southern Railway, which already had two other members of the class in use on the Lyme Regis branch. This locomotive has been preserved on the Bluebell Railway in East Sussex.

No 6 was an 'O'-class 0-6-0 goods locomotive built in 1893 by Sharp, Stewart & Co for the South Eastern Railway and was later given an 'O1'-class boiler while retaining an original Stirling cab and smokebox. Purchased by the EKR in 1923, it survived into British Railways days, being withdrawn in 1949. No 7 was an 'E0330'-class 0-6-0ST built by Beyer Peacock in 1882 for the LSWR; purchased in 1924 from the Southern Railway, it was withdrawn in 1941. No 8 was a second 'O'-class 0-6-0, built for the SER in 1893 by Sharp, Stewart. Purchased from the SR in 1928, it was found to be in poor condition and was withdrawn in 1934.

No 100 (later numbered 2) was an 'O1' 0-6-0 goods built as an 'O' for the SER by Sharp, Stewart in 1893. Purchased in rebuilt condition in 1935, it survived into BR days, until 1955. The last locomotive purchased by the EKR was a further 'O1' built as an 'O' for the SER by Sharp, Stewart, in 1891, and had been numbered 1317 by the Southern Railway. Purchased in 1944, it was withdrawn by BR in 1949.

The EKR had an interesting variety of rolling stock, including carriages from the London, Chatham & Dover Railway, the London & South Western Railway, the North London Railway, the Great Eastern Railway and the Cheshire Lines Committee. Its first bogie carriage was an ex-KESR brake vehicle built in 1904 for the latter's Headcorn extension; this carriage was acquired in 1912 for the opening of the line and was used for inspection work until the EKR opened to passenger traffic in 1916. The final two carriages to be acquired were also bogie vehicles, built by the LSWR as Second-class corridor stock. Acquired from the SR in 1946, both were scrapped in 1948 after the line closed to passenger traffic. The remainder of the carriage stock was made up of four- and six-wheel vehicles. Equally the company had an interesting variety of goods rolling stock purchased from the London, Brighton & South Coast Railway, the Midland Railway, the London, Midland & Scottish Railway, the LSWR and the SECR. In addition there were a large number of open wagons built by private wagon-builders.

Right: Adams 4-4-2 radial tank No 5 (ex-LSWR No 488) together with Kerr Stuart 0-6-0T No 4 at Shepherdswell shed on 18 July 1936. No 5 would be sold to the Southern Railway in 1946, in order to provide a third Adams radial tank on the Lyme Regis branch, which was very short of suitable motive power. No 4 owned by the local coal syndicate but became British Railways property in 1948, following which it was withdrawn and scrapped. *H. C. Casserley*

Right: A line-up of odd locomotives at Shepherdswell shed *c*1927. From left to right are ex-LSWR 'Ilfracombe' 0-6-0 No 394, East Kent Railway No 3 in a part-dismantled state, KESR 2-4-0T No 2 *Northiam* on hire and 'O'-class 0-6-0 No 6. Note the bank of water tanks behind the locomotives. *H. C. Casserley*

Left: Eythorne station looking well-kempt when viewed in the direction of Shepherdswell on 2 September 1938. This station consisted of a brick building on a timber-and-ash platform and had full signalling. *Roger Carpenter*

Below: The same location nearly 20 years later, *circa* July 1958, with the station building closed and boarded up and the platform shortened by two and a half carriage lengths. *J. H. Aston*

Above: 'O1' 0-6-0 No 31434 heads
a coal train from Tilmanstone
Colliery up the bank to the
exchange sidings at Shepherdswell
on 24 April 1959. *R. F. Roberts*

Right: Golgotha Tunnel *c*1958. This
photograph, taken in the direction of
Tilmanstone Colliery, shows clearly the
width of the tunnel, which, despite being
built to accommodate two tracks, only
ever had a single track laid through it.
*Pamlin Prints / R. M. Casserley
collection*

Below: Tilmanstone Colliery shortly after
opening, with a wide variety of wagons,
some from as far away as Scotland.
R. M. Casserley collection

Left: Elvington station, with its small shelter built on a brick platform, pictured on 2 September 1938. *Roger Carpenter*

Left: A desolate Eastry South, viewed in the direction of Canterbury Road in the summer of 1938. *Author's collection*

Below: 0-6-0ST No 2 heads a train of ex-LCDR stock across the bridge at Eastry on its journey to Canterbury Road *c*1938. *Author's collection*

Left: Taken in the direction of Shepherdswell on 15 September 1936, this photograph of Eastry station provides a good view of the brick platform and timber-hut station building. Note also the full signalling and the heavy flat-bottom rails. *J. H. L. Adams*

Right: Woodnesborough station *c*1935, viewed in the direction of Shepherdswell. Although the station building was smaller than that at Eastry, the platform had iron railings and was lit by oil lamps. *Author's collection*

Left: Staple & Ash station, with its brick building and platform, viewed in the direction of Wingham in August 1937. This station featured a wind pump and water tank, as well as a siding with a brick-built loading platform. Staple was also home to one of the railway's few industrial customers, C. W. Darley Ltd, which had a warehouse next to the station. *Roger Carpenter*

Right: A second view of Staple station, this time recorded on 2 September 1938 in the direction of Shepherdswell, showing the brick-built goods platform (right) and, on the opposite platform, the grounded carriage body used as an office. *Roger Carpenter*

Above: An early picture of Wingham Town station, taken c1920, showing the timber building and brick-built platforms. Hudswell Clarke 0-6-0ST No 2 *Walton Park* calls with a single-carriage train consisting of ex LSWR six-wheel Brake Third No 5. Wingham Town was the terminus of the line before the extension to Canterbury Road, opened in 1925. *Author's collection*

Below: Locomotive No 2, formerly *Walton Park* but now minus nameplates, coupled to a solitary ex-LCDR six-wheel Brake third in the siding at Wingham Canterbury Road while preparing for a return run to Shepherdswell in June 1939. *A. W. V. Mace*

Above: The second No 2, an 'O1' 0-6-0 acquired from the SR in 1935 and initially numbered 100, at Canterbury Wingham Road on 5 June 1948, just months before the cessation of passenger services. On the right, one of the ex-LSWR bogie corridor Brake First/Third carriages is being gravity-shunted into the station platform. *P. J. Garland*

Right: An early photograph of Wingham Canterbury Road station, taken *c*1925, shortly after opening to traffic and showing the basic timber building, waiting bench for any potential passengers and the line towards Canterbury, ending in a pile of sleepers and an old wagon. The timber-built platform, with corrugated-iron face and ash surface, tends to confirm the status of this temporary terminus serving little more than a field. *Ian Allan Library*

Right: Wingham Canterbury Road station photographed in the direction of Shepherdswell near the end of its existence, on 25 April 1947. *H. C. Casserley*

Above: Poison Cross station, on the Richborough Harbour branch, viewed in the direction of Richborough in the autumn on 2 September 1938. Although the line was still used for goods traffic, passenger services had ceased a decade earlier, on 31 October 1928.
Roger Carpenter

Left: A very bleak-looking Roman Road station, viewed in the direction of Richborough *c*1930, a few years after the last passenger train had departed.
Author's collection

Left: For a few short years, from August 1925 until October 1928, the Richborough branch saw passenger trains, as this rare photograph bears witness. Ex-LSWR 0-6-0ST No 7 heads a pair of six-wheel carriages — the first being EKR No 5, also acquired from the LSWR, the second an ex-Midland vehicle — at Sandwich Road station on 23 September 1928.
R. M. Casserley collection

Right: Sandwich Road station viewed in the direction of Richborough c1928, with the ticket hut and nameboard still *in situ* on the ash platform. This was the limit of passenger operation, as the EKR never gained permission to run such services to Richborough Port over two very suspect bridges. The block section from Poison Cross to Sandwich Road was officially labelled on the train staff as 'Poison–Sandwich'! *Author's collection*

Right: The basic and rickety single-track bridge across the Dover–Ramsgate main line near Richborough. Little wonder the East Kent Railway could not get permission to run passenger trains over this spindly structure. *Colonel Stephens Museum, Tenterden*

Below: The second rickety bridge, this one over the River Stour, photographed in July 1937 in the direction of Richborough Port. *R. F. Roberts*

Below right: The station that never saw a passenger. Richborough Port, complete with nameboard and passenger seat, on 2 September 1938. The line in the foreground was part of the port system, by then owned by Pearson Dorman Long, which was less than keen to negotiate an agreement with the East Kent Railway. *Roger Carpenter*

THE SHEPPEY LIGHT RAILWAY

The county of Kent has a long coastline, from the East Sussex boundary near Rye to the outskirts of London near Greenwich. Probably the bleakest and, at times, most haunting stretch is that facing north across the Thames Estuary towards the Essex coast, in which lies the Isle of Sheppey. This is not far from the marshy area so vividly described by Charles Dickens in his novel *Great Expectations*. A bleak, cold and remote area, full of bogs and reeds, it nevertheless possesses an eerie beauty.

Although there was little in this part of the county to attract the main-line railway companies, ribbons of branch lines were planned as long ago as the mid-19th century, but it was not until the 1860s, when the rival London, Chatham & Dover and South Eastern railways ventured into the area, that the situation began to improve for the local population.

The development of Sheerness by the LCDR and the later opening (in 1875) of Queensborough Pier, with its ferry service to Flushing, in Holland, changed the face of this remote area, and there was considerable rivalry for this lucrative Continental traffic from the South Eastern Railway at Port Victoria. However, the main line ran along the west coast of the Isle of Sheppey from Sittingbourne to Sheerness Dockyard, and the rest of the island did not benefit from a rail connection. By the late 19th century the local populace were feeling left out of things and that a rail connection with the main line and London was desirable. Holman Fred Stephens was involved with this arrangement from the start, through his friendship with Lord Medway, who gave him a letter of introduction to Lord Harris of Belmont Park, an influential local landowner.

The original plan was for a line running south from Queensborough station, across the marshes to the south of the island almost in a straight line, bypassing all the centres of population and terminating at Leysdown. However, following a Public Enquiry held by the Light Railway Commission at Queensborough on 29 April 1898 it was decided to build the line across the north of the island, taking in all the main areas of habitation.

The Sheppey Light Railway was promoted by the newly formed Light Railway Syndicate headed by Edward I. W. Peterson, a solicitor and friend of Stephens whom he had met during the construction of the Paddock Wood & Hawkhurst line. The contractor was William Rigby, who was responsible for all the work on the line, which duly opened for traffic on 1 August 1901.

The stations were a mixture of styles ranging from full station buildings in the Stephens style in the main areas of population to the rather basic timber halts in lesser areas. The line had basic signalling at main stations, and gates protected a number of the level crossings, although a proportion of the latter followed the light-railway tradition of ungated crossings.

The line saw a wide variety of motive power over the years. At the time of the opening in 1901 the SECR, which had the contract to operate the line, allocated ex-LCDR 'Scotchmen' 0-4-2 well-tank

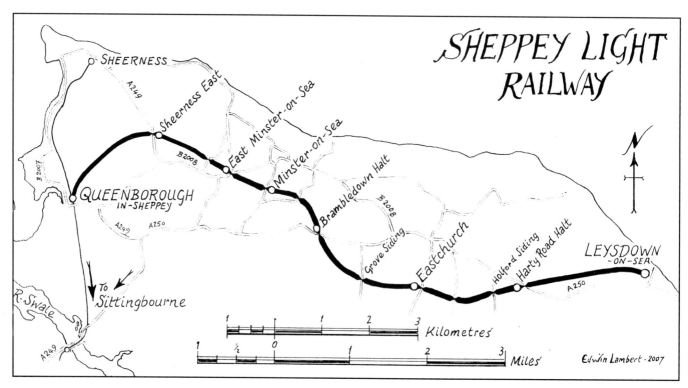

locomotives built in 1866 by Neilson, and these were joined by the 'Sonders'-class 2-4-0Ts built in 1857 by R. & W. Hawthorn. In 1903, in an attempt to reduce operating costs, a trial was conducted using Dick, Kerr petrol railcars, and in 1905 these were followed by Kitson steam railcars, of which Nos 1 and 5 remained in use until the outbreak of the Great War in 1914.

One notable locomotive that ran on the line was an ex-LBSCR Class A1 'Terrier' 0-6-0 tank, No 654 *Waddon*, which after purchase by the SECR and repainting in full Wainwright lined green became No 751 and was nicknamed 'Little Tich', after the music-hall artist Harry Relph, who had been born in Kent and was very popular in the Edwardian era. This locomotive, which as No DS680 lasted in use until 1963 at Lancing Carriage Works, near Brighton, is nowadays preserved at the Montreal Railway Museum in Canada.

During and after the Great War trains on the Sheppey Light Railway were worked by various types, notably 'P'-class 0-6-0Ts, 'O1' 0-6-0s and, in the early 1920s, 'Q'-class 0-4-4Ts. After the 1923 Grouping the line settled down to using LCDR 'R1' 0-4-4 tanks and the occasional visiting 'F1'-class 4-4-0 on passenger services. There were also visits by 'D'-class 4-4-0s on special trains until closure in 1950, while 'C'-class 0-6-0s worked goods and, at times, some passenger services.

The original carriage stock comprised LCDR four- and six-wheelers, which were replaced by the petrol railcars on trial, themselves replaced by Kitson steam railcars; after these were withdrawn during the Great War the service reverted to four- and six-wheel carriage stock. In the 1920s the railcar carriage bodies returned in the form of articulated carriage sets, which worked on the line until closure in 1950, after which they were used on the Clapham Junction–Kensington Addison Road service.

The railway ran across the northern part of the island from a bay platform at Queensborough via Sheerness East, EastMinster-on-Sea, Minster-on-Sea, Brambledown Halt, Eastchurch and Harty Road before reaching the terminus at Leysdown. There were sidings at Grove and at Halford, halfway along the line. Although in many respects the line led a quiet day-to-day existence, there were highlights when times became more exciting. During the Great War a school of aviation was established at Eastchurch, with its own sidings, for which the SECR was responsible. In September 1917 a bomb landed on the line near Sheerness East station, stopping the service all day.

In 1938 the Southern Railway proposed building a holiday camp at Leysdown to accommodate the many campers who visited the Isle of Sheppey in the summer. However, with war clouds looming this came to nought, as had an earlier plan for an hotel. The line soldiered on through World War 2, serving the local community, but in the postwar era its economic prospects were bleak.

Following nationalisation of the railways in 1948 the newly created British Railways was quick to rid itself of uneconomic lines, and, despite protests from local councils, the decision was taken to close the SLR with effect from Monday 4 December 1950. In fact the last train ran on Saturday 2 December ,when the line was given a rousing send-off from locals as well as visitors, many of whom travelled many miles to bid it a final farewell.

Below: View of the main station building and booking hall at Queenborough *c*1959, showing the distinctive design with pointed gables and high-pitched roof. *Author's collection*

Left: As a 'C'-class 0-6-0 departs Queenborough in the direction of Sheerness with a three-car set of 'birdcage' stock, the train for Leysdown stands at the bay platform, awaiting the guard's whistle. The photograph was taken in *c*1949. *Author's collection*

Below: SECR Kitson steam railmotor No 1 arriving at Queenborough station *c*1901. *P. A. Harding collection*

Bottom: 'R1' 0-4-4T No 31674 arrives at Queenborough with an articulated carriage set from Leysdown in the summer of 1949. *H. J. P. Rutherford*

Top right: 'R1' 0-4-4T No 31696 coasts into the station at Sheerness East with a train for Queenborough in the summer of 1950. *P. Ransome-Wallis*

Above right: 'C'-class 0-6-0 No 1252 crosses the road at Scropes Gate, near Minster-on-Sea, with a train for Queenborough on 2 June 1936. *H. F. Wheeler*

Right: Brambledown Halt basks in the summer sunshine *c*1930, showing no sign of passengers or activity. *P. A. Harding collection*

Top: The level-crossing gates at Brambledown Halt are opened by the train guard as 'C'-class 0-6-0 No 1252 awaits the 'right away' to Leysdown on 2 June 1936.
H. F. Wheeler

Above: Towards the end of the line's existence, in the summer of 1950, an 'R1' 0-4-4T and an articulated carriage set forming a service to Queenborough arrive at Eastchurch station. *R. M. Casserley*

Left: A lonely-looking Harty Road Halt glints in summer sunshine *c*1930.
Author's collection

Above: A contrasting scene recorded at Leysdown *c*1950, revealing how bleak the North Kent coast can be in the depths of winter. *Author's collection*

Right: 'C'-class 0-6-0 No 1252 prepares to depart Leysdown for Queenborough on 2 June 1936 with an articulated set and a van for any heavy luggage or parcels. *H. F. Wheeler*

Below: 'R1'-class 0-4-4T No 1673 departs Leysdown station with a service for Queenborough in the winter of 1947. *P. Ransome-Wallis*

Top: In full BR lined black but with lion-and-wheel totem yet to be applied, 'R1' 0-4-4T No 31698 leaves Leysdown for Queenborough on 4 February 1950. The photograph shows clearly the run-round loop, sidings and pointwork at this station. *Pamlin Prints*

Above: Close-up of bogie articulated set No 514, at Leysdown on 2 June 1936, showing how neatly the carriage portions of the ex-SECR Kitson steam railmotors were rebuilt. Note also the Maunsell short-wheelbase 12-ton van at the rear. *H. F. Wheeler*

Left: A detailed photograph of the articulated bogie, showing how the carriage bodies were attached. *H. F. Wheeler*

Right: Interior view of one of the articulated carriages, showing the seating arrangements and internal décor. *H. F. Wheeler*

Below right: Trains on the Sheppey Light Railway were run as an early form of 'paytrain', with the guard taking fares and issuing tickets. *H. F. Wheeler*

Bottom right: LBSCR 'Terrier' No 654 *Waddon*, which was sold to the SECR in 1901 for use on the Sheppey Light Railway, where it was used for a time to work goods services. It was later used in a number of other locations, ending up as the Lancing Carriage Works shunter (No DS680) before being purchased privately for restoration and export (in 1964) to Canada, where it can now be seen at the Railway Museum in Montreal, Quebec, in full Stroudley yellow livery. This photograph, taken *c*1919, shows the locomotive as SECR No 751 in dark-grey wartime livery. *Author's collection*

Below: Closure notice for the Sheppey Light Railway *c*1951. *Author's collection*

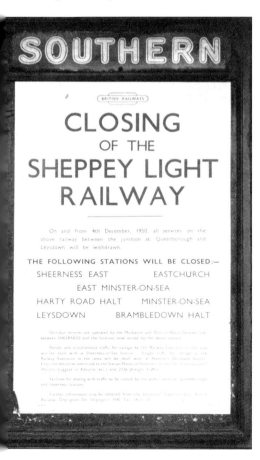

SOUTHERN

BRITISH RAILWAYS

CLOSING
OF THE
SHEPPEY LIGHT RAILWAY

On and from 4th December, 1950, all services on the above railway between the junction at Queenborough and Leysdown will be withdrawn.

THE FOLLOWING STATIONS WILL BE CLOSED:—

SHEERNESS EAST   EASTCHURCH

EAST MINSTER-ON-SEA

HARTY ROAD HALT   MINSTER-ON-SEA

LEYSDOWN   BRAMBLEDOWN HALT

THE HAWKHURST BRANCH

No other branch line featured in this book better typifies the railway byways of Kent than does the Hawkhurst branch. In common with the neighbouring Kent & East Sussex Railway, the Hawkhurst line was the work of Lt Col Holman Fred Stephens, who as Resident Engineer was responsible to the line's Consulting Engineer, Edward Seaton.

The line was promoted by the South Eastern Railway as the Cranbrook & Paddock Wood Railway in 1877, when an Act was passed to build the line from Paddock Wood, on the Tonbridge–Ashford line, to Cranbrook. Further powers were obtained in 1882 to extend the railway to Gills Green, a mile north of Hawkhurst, making the branch 11½ miles long.

This was the first line with which Stephens was involved, and as a result he made a number of important contacts that would be of value to him in the future. It was during this project, for instance, that the young Stephens met William Henry Austen, who in later years took over the management of lines that he had created. He also came into contact with Mancktelow Bros, of Horsmonden, which firm had much to do with the construction work on many of the Stephens lines in the late 19th and early 20th centuries. The other important contact made at this time was that of Joseph Fairbank, who was involved with a number of early Stephens railways.

The first section of the Hawkhurst branch, from Paddock Wood via Horsmonden to Hope Mill (Goudhurst), was opened on 12 September 1892, Cranbrook and Hawkhurst were reached on 4 September 1893; at this time also Hope Mill was renamed Goudhurst. The original intention was to continue the line to Appledore, but this never came to anything. In the early 1900s there were also proposals to build a connection from Rolvenden, on the Kent & East Sussex Railway, to Cranbrook, but, again, these got no further than the planning stage.

The branch was built to main-line standards, with full signalling and heavy permanent way. The stations were built by Mancktelow Bros to a design that became standard on the Stephens railways, with corrugated-iron walls and roof, with an awning and supports at the front. They had full goods facilities and could handle a high level of traffic, while those at Goudhurst and Cranbrook had substantial brick-built three-storey stationmaster's houses. At Hawkhurst stood a locomotive shed, which was used for only a short time but still survives today, along with the signalbox.

At the time of the line's opening in the late 1890s there was no road competition, so it made a reasonable profit, but after the Great War its fortune started to decline as a result of competition from

Below: 'H'-class 0-4-4T No 31520 simmers in the bay at Paddock Wood station on 15 July 1960, awaiting the signal to start its journey to Hawkhurst through some of the most beautiful countryside in the whole of Britain. The two-car pull-push set to the left is the branch's spare carriage set, No 715.
J. Grant collection

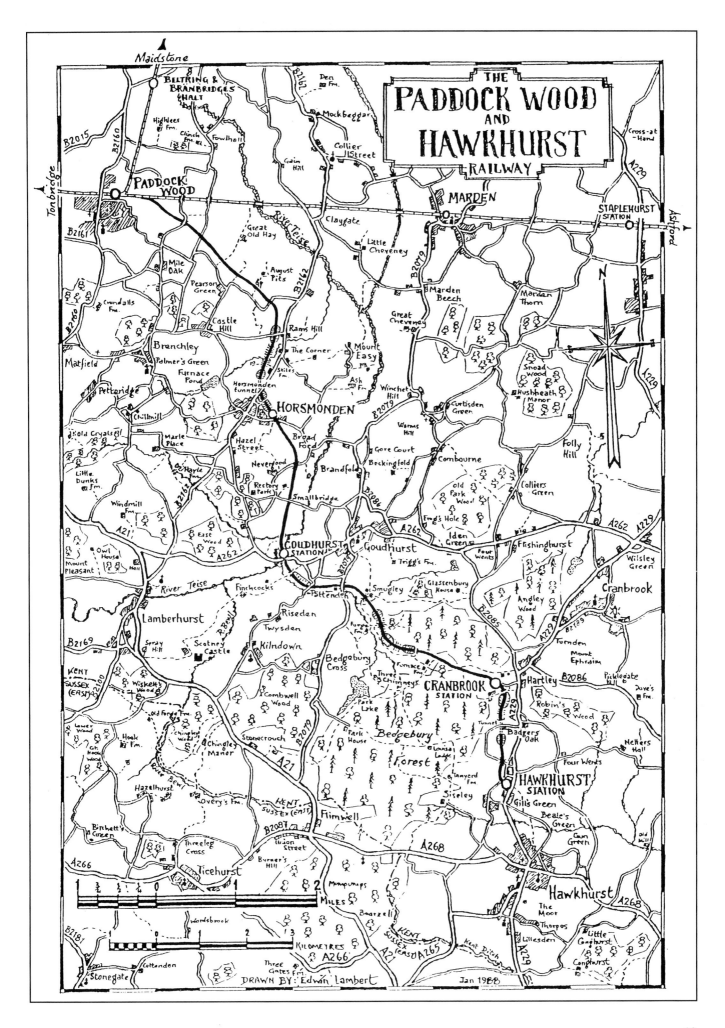

bus and road-haulage companies, which reduced profits over the years. However, one important feature remained the hop-pickers' trains, which ran on Sundays when there was no normal service. These ran from Cannon Street and Charing Cross, bringing the hop-pickers, their families and friends down to Kent to harvest the yearly crop of hops. The pickers were mainly east and south Londoners, for whom this was often their only holiday and their only chance to escape the dirt and grime of the poorer parts of London. The hop-picking holidays came to an end in the late 1950s, when most growers of hops invested in machines to harvest the crop.

During its lifetime the Hawkhurst branch saw a wide variety of locomotives. At the time of the opening to Hope Mill in 1892 Cudworth 'E'-class 2-4-0s were used on the passenger trains, and Cudworth standard 0-6-0s on the pick-up goods, both types being outside-frame designs. In the years immediately prior to the Great War they were replaced respectively by 'Q'-class 0-4-4 tanks and 'O'-class 0-6-0s, and by the early 1920s passenger trains were worked additionally by 4-4-0s of Classes B and F.

After the formation in 1923 of the Southern Railway the branch reverted to a mixture of 'Q'-class 0-4-4Ts on passenger trains and 'C'-class 0-6-0s on goods. After the former were withdrawn *en masse* in the early 1930s passenger services were worked by ex-LBSCR 'D1' 0-4-2 and, at times, 'D3' 0-4-4 tank engines. During this period Brighton 'E4' 0-6-2 tanks were also employed on goods trains, supplementing the 'O1' 0-6-0s.

There were some unusual allocations over the years, including the SECR 0-6-0ST No 752 from Folkestone Quay, built as a contractor's locomotive by Manning, Wardle and nicknamed 'Thumper' by the crews. In 1936 the Sentinel bogie steam railcar was tried on the line, without success, and the 'C'-class 0-6-0s and 'R1' 0-4-4Ts remained the staple motive power until the mid-1950s, when 'H'-class 0-4-4Ts replaced the 'R1s' on passenger services. During this time special train services — principally Saturday and Sunday extras for hop-pickers and Benenden Girls' School — were handled by passenger 4-4-0s of the 'D', 'D1', 'E1' and, occasionally, 'L' classes. For a time in the late 1950s a 350hp diesel shunter, based at Paddock Wood, was used in place of the usual

'C'-class 0-6-0 to work the pick-up goods to Hawkhurst, but it was found that steam was faster and more reliable on this work.

Carriage stock consisted originally of SER four- and six-wheel stock. From 1899 this was replaced by early London, Chatham & Dover Railway bogie stock, which following the Grouping in 1923 gave way to a mixture of SECR, LBSCR and LSWR bogie stock; this included LSWR pull-push sets, which lasted until 1958, after which rebuilt Maunsell two-car pull-push sets were used until closure. In the late 1950s British Railways looked at the possibility of using 'Hampshire' two-car diesel-electric multiple-units, but this came to nothing.

The Hawkhurst branch lasted with only minor changes through the 1920s and 1930s despite declining traffic and it served the local area during the dark days of World War 2. However, with peace and the cold reality of postwar Britain its fortunes declined further, until by the late 1950s, following the loss of more local traffic, BR Southern Region regarded closure as the only realistic option.

In truth this was partly engineered by the then powers that be, by juggling the accounts to justify the line's demise. With Phase 2 of the Kent Coast electrification it was felt that branches like Hawkhurst and Westerham were an inconvenience and did not fit in with the image of the swish new motive power. The Hawkhurst branch would have made an ideal tourist line and today would have put Hawkhurst and the villages along the route within easy reach of a day or weekend trip, but this was not to be, and, despite local protest, the railway closed to all traffic on Saturday 10 June 1961. The following day a special last train down the branch, the 'South Eastern Limited', organised by the Locomotive Club of Great Britain and headed by 'C'-class 0-6-0 No 31592 and 'O1' No 31065, marked the end of steam on the South Eastern division of the Southern Region.

On at least two occasions British Railways tried to persuade the members of the fledgling Kent & East Sussex Railway Association to divert their attentions to the Hawkhurst branch, but to no avail. The branch was lifted in 1964, and, apart from station buildings at Horsmonden and Cranbrook and the locomotive shed and signalbox at Hawkhurst, little now remains of this lovely Kent byway.

Left: Goudhurst started life as Hope Mill station in 1892 and was renamed when the branch reached Hawkhurst, on 4 September 1893. Hops were always an important traffic along the line, as were the hop-pickers who came from East and South East London to harvest the annual crop. A hop-pickers' excursion headed by a 'C'-class 0-6-0, No 31717, and a 'D'-class 4-4-0, No 31739, runs into the station with a return Sunday working to London on 29 September 1951. The branch was usually closed on Sundays save during the hop-picking season. *Pamlin Prints / R. M. Casserley collection*

Left: 'Having arrived with the daily pick-up goods from Cranbrook, 'C'-class 0-6-0 No 31592 waits to shunt the goods yard at Goudhurst before proceeding to Horsmonden on Tuesday 2 May 1961, barely a month before closure of the line. *E. A. Woollard*

Below left: Not a scene from *The Great St Trinian's Train Robbery* but the aftermath of a derailment on 18 February 1948, when 'C'-class 0-6-0 No 1225 was wrongly despatched into the north sidings at Goudhurst. *G. W. Batchelor*

Above right: Ex-LBSCR 'E4' 0-6-2T No 32580 arrives at Cranbrook on 10 August 1955 with the 1.50pm goods from Paddock Wood, which included an ex-works pull-push unit (No 721) on its way to Hawkhurst. *J. H. Aston*

Right: A panoramic view of Cranbrook station on 29 September 1951, showing the buildings, track layout and signalling. *Lens of Sutton collection*

Above: An aerial view of Hawkhurst *c*1955, clearly showing the trackwork and the layout of the buildings. At the top of the picture is the locomotive depot, by now out of use, while at the centre is the goods shed, and in the bottom left the coal yard, next to the station. *J. Grant collection*

Above left: Ex-South Eastern & Chatham Railway 'F'-class 4-4-0 No A458 prepares to head a train of ex-LCDR six-wheel stock on a service from Hawkhurst to Paddock Wood on 17 July 1926. The Hawkhurst branch enjoyed a wide variety of locomotives at this time. *H. C. Casserley*

Left: 'H'-class 0-4-4T No 31543 makes a spirited start from Cranbrook station with a pull-push train to Hawkhurst *c*1959. *J. Grant collection*

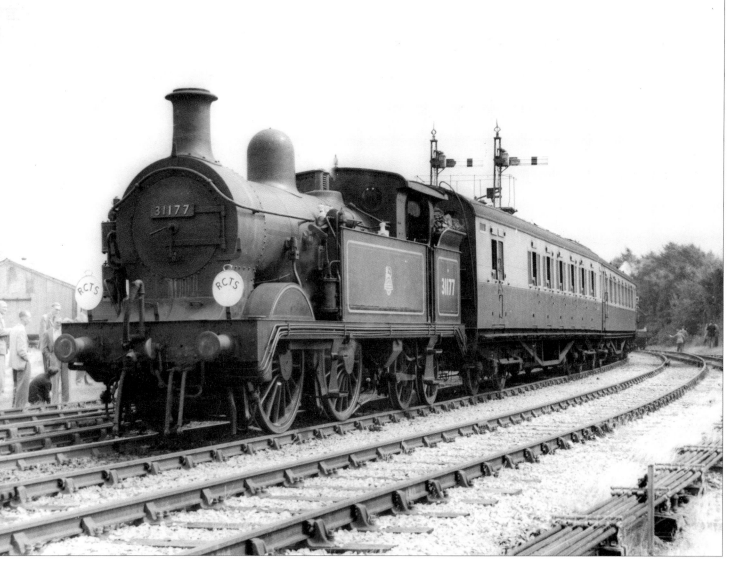

Above: 'H'-class 0-4-4T No 31177 at Hawkhurst on 12 June 1955 with a special train of Maunsell bogie stock in carmine and cream. Such specials, run for enthusiasts or ramblers, would often traverse the line on Saturdays or Sundays. *E. E. Smith*

Below left: A general view of Hawkhurst station on 15 July 1958, with the signalbox, water tower and locomotive shed in full view. The carriage stock on the right consists of LBSCR and SECR bogie non-corridor vehicles converted for pull-push working. *H. F. Wheeler*

Below right: The ex-SER ground signal controlling the loop at Hawkhurst station, pictured *c*1962, a year after closure. *J. Knapman*

Above: The goods yard at Hawkhurst *c*1960, with vans awaiting plant and flower traffic for Woolworth's, which at that time had contracts with several local growers. This area later became part of the local timber yard.
R. K. Blencowe collection

Left: A photograph of Hawkhurst station taken in May 1961, only a month before closure, showing the newly painted building and the stop blocks at the end of the line. *E. E. Banks*

Right: Viewed from the bay end of the platform, having arrived behind an 'H'-class tank, pull-push set No 739 stands at Hawkhurst on 15 July 1958. *H. F. Wheeler*

THE PORT VICTORIA & ALL HALLOWS BRANCH

Like the Isle of Sheppey, the Isle of Grain and the Hundred of Hoo Peninsula constitute a lonely, almost ghostly part of the north Kent coast, and today it is difficult to imagine that not so long ago this remote area had a railway network connecting Gravesend Central via a junction near Milton Ranges Halt to the far end of the peninsula at Port Victoria, as well as a branch from Stoke Junction Halt to All Hallows-on-Sea.

The main reason for a railway in such a remote area of Kent was the rivalry between the South Eastern and London, Chatham & Dover railways. In 1876 the LCDR opened a branch from its Sheerness branch to Queensborough Pier and started to run a cross Channel packet service to Flushing in Holland. This prompted the SER to support a project to build a line, promoted by the Hundred of Hoo Railway Company, across the Isle of Grain from a junction near Shorne Marshes to Stoke. A decade earlier, in 1865, a local group had tried to promote a railway along a similar route, but despite gaining Parliamentary assent the project had foundered in the face of opposition from both the SER and the LCDR.

The railway was authorised on 21 July 1879, and from the start the SER agreed to operate the single-track branch and also to make available funds for the construction of a line from Stoke to Queensborough Pier, to connect with a proposed steam-packet service to France. In 1881 the Hundred of Hoo Railway Co was taken over by the SER. Engineer for the project was Francis Brady, who, together with contractor George Furness, constructed the North Kent Railway near Milton to Stoke. The remainder of the line to Port Victoria was constructed by T. A. Walker. The line from Hoo to Sharnal Street was opened on 1 April 1882, to be followed on 11 September 1882 by that to Port Victoria. At first the pier at Port Victoria was not a total success, the only ferry service being to Sheerness, but this changed in 1882 with the introduction of the steam-packet service to France.

The cross-Channel route via Port Victoria found favour with the Royal Family often being used for official journeys to the Continent as well as by foreign heads of state for official visits to England. Indeed, such was the popularity of Port Victoria that the Royal Corinthian Yacht Club was based there from 1899. Shortly after the formation in that same year of the South Eastern & Chatham Joint Committee the pier at Queensborough burned down, with the result that the steamers on the Flushing service had to use Port Victoria until Queensborough Pier was rebuilt.

In 1906, in a bid to improve the fortunes of the branch, a number of timber halts were constructed between Hoo Junction and Port Victoria, at Uralite, High Halstow, Beluncle, Middle Stoke and Stoke Junction.

During the Great War Port Victoria served as a base for the Royal Navy and was used by warships patrolling the Thames Estuary, as well as by seaplanes of the Royal Naval Air Service, to counteract submarine and zeppelin attacks on Chatham and London.

The steam-packet service was a casualty of the Great War, and by 1916 the pier at Port Victoria had become structurally unsafe; trains no longer called at the pier station, instead using a new platform just short of the pier. The station building on the pier was formally closed in 1932, replaced by a second new platform built by the Southern Railway, which had taken over at the Grouping in 1923.

By the late 1920s a sizeable proportion of Britain's population was opting to take its annual week's holiday on the South Coast, Kent being a popular destination, and the Southern Railway's marketing department had the idea of creating a new holiday resort on the north coast of the Isle of Grain. Built on land reclaimed from the mud of the Thames Estuary, All Hallows-on-Sea comprised little but an art-deco pub, a few guest houses, a couple of shops and a large quantity of builder's sand. It was served by a branch — authorised in June 1929 and built under the direction of Resident

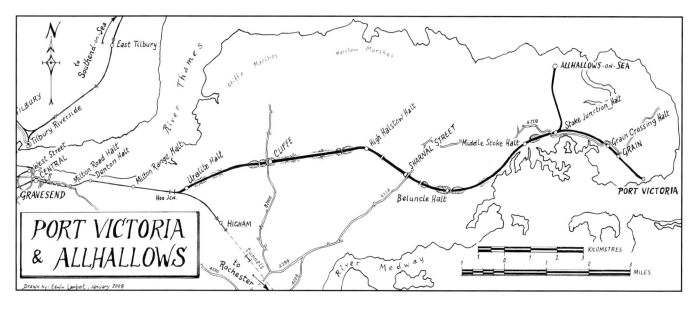

Engineer R. C. Coward — from what became known as Stoke Junction, between Middle Stoke and Grain Crossing Halt. Single-track at the time of its opening on 14 May 1932, the line was doubled in 1934, while the station at All Hallows, close to the seafront and the art-deco pub, was a modern Walker-period affair with an island platform, complete with canopy — all this at a time when the Southern had a real tourist attraction in the form of the narrow-gauge Lynton & Barnstaple line in north Devon, which it never advertised or promoted and was ultimately quite happy to close.

Unsurprisingly the new resort at All Hallows did not take off, and in the interwar period the branch from Hoo Junction witnessed a slow but steady decline. This continued until the outbreak of World War 2 in September 1939, when the area around Port Victoria was taken over by an oil company and an oil refinery and oil-storage facility were built. During the war the line found a new lease of life transporting the products of the refinery and providing a passenger service for the workers at the expanding plant. However, things were not as rosy as the Southern Railway (and, subsequently, British Railways' Southern Region) might have hoped, and from the end of World War 2 passenger numbers declined year by year as the oil-refinery workers started to travel to work by bus and, later, by car. Following the opening of a new platform at Grain, both the station at Port Victoria and the halt at Grain Crossing closed with effect from 10 June 1951.

Postwar the SR also lost faith in All Hallows, which from the late 1940s generated dwindling returns. By the late 1950s British Railways was looking to make economies by closing loss-making lines, and in 1957 the section from Stoke Junction was singled. However, this was not enough to save it, and following consultation, involving some quite heated debate with local councils, closure was sanctioned to take effect from 2 December 1961, this applying also to all the stations along the line from Hoo Junction.

Over the years the branch from Hoo Junction saw a wide variety of motive power. Before and just after the Great War this comprised 4-4-0s of Classes D, D1, E, E1 and F, while tank engines ranged from 'Q' and 'Q1' to 'R' and 'R1' 0-4-4Ts, joined in the post-WW2 era by 'H'-class 0-4-4Ts. 'C'-, 'O1'- and, latterly, 'Q1'-class 0-6-0 tender engines were used on the pick-up goods services. In later years, from the late 1930s until withdrawal of services in the 1950s and '60s, passenger trains were composed of pull-push units and Maunsell and, latterly, Bulleid carriage sets.

The line from Hoo Junction to Grain remains open, seeing a large tonnage of aggregate, cement and concrete traffic (although the oil refinery has contracted in the last few decades), and since 1960 has been worked by diesel locomotives of Classes 33, 37, 47, 60 and, most recently, 66. By contrast the section between the site of Stoke Halt and All Hallows-on-Sea is no more, and today it is difficult to find any trace of the ill-fated branch to the holiday resort that never was.

Above: 'H'-class 0-4-4T No 31177 waits with its pull-push motor set in the centre road at Gravesend Central before dropping back into the platform to form the next train to All Hallows-on-Sea on 14 May 1960. *H. C. Casserley.*

Right: A second view of Gravesend Central, this time on 11 March 1961, with the All Hallows-on-Sea train, made up of pull-push set No 657, waiting at the platform. *H. C. Casserley*

Above: In the early 1950s an experimental three-car DMU set built by ACV spent a short time on the All Hallows branch, being seen here at Gravesend Central on 24 October 1953. *R. C. Riley*

Left: The bleak concrete platform at Hoo Junction, pictured on 14 May 1960. This served the goods yard behind and was for the use of railway staff only. *H. C. Casserley*

Below: The original timber-built Uralite Halt as opened during the days of the Kitson steam railmotors, just before the Great War. *Lens of Sutton collection*

Top: The replacement Uralite Halt, built by the SR in the 1930s using parts supplied by Exmouth Concrete Works. The factory it was designed to serve can be seen in the background. *R. M. Casserley*

Above: View of Cliffe station *c*1935, showing the buildings and track layout. Most of the important stations on the branch had passing-loops and full signalling. *Lens of Sutton collection*

Right: The ACV experimental railcar set on the 1.45pm All Hallows service passes the 2.25pm Gravesend service at Cliffe on 24 October 1953. *R. C. Riley*

Above: A member of railway staff waits expectantly as 'H'-class 0-4-4T No 31322 coasts into the platform at High Halstow Halt on 9 July 1955. *J. H. Aston*

Left: En route to Gravesend Central from All Hallows-on-Sea, 'H'-class 0-4-4T No 31308 and Brighton pull-push set No 753 make their way through the bleak expanses surrounding Sharnal Street station c1958. The line in the foreground is the station passing-loop, while on the far right can be seen the exchange sidings for the 2ft 6in-gauge Chattenden & Upnor Railway, serving the Royal Navy's ordinance depot. *Lens of Sutton collection*

Below: The 12.05pm All Hallows-on-Sea–Gravesend service, headed by 'H'-class 0-4-4T No 31520, at Sharnal Street on Good Friday (3 April) 1953. The Mk 1 corridor set, in carmine-and-cream livery, had been used for an excursion earlier that morning and was being employed on a filling-in turn before working the return leg of the excursion from All Hallows. *Derek Cross*

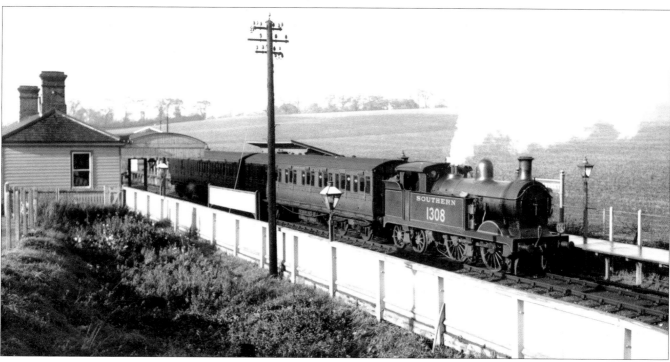

Top: Sharnal Street station on 20 October 1951, viewed in the direction of Gravesend Central. The photograph shows the track layout, as well as the timber-and-brick station buildings and the timber-built shelter on the platform opposite. *Lens of Sutton collection*

Above: Heading a Brighton pull-push set bound for All Hallows-on-Sea, 'H'-class 0-4-4T No 1308 is illuminated by weak winter sunshine at Sharnal Street *c*1935. *Lens of Sutton collection*

Right: Beluncle Halt *c*1924, still in its original form as a timber-built halt used by steam railmotors, before the Southern Railway rebuilt it with a concrete platform. *Lens of Sutton collection*

Left: View of Middle Stoke Halt *c*1959, showing the kit-built construction of the basic concrete waiting hut and platform with steel railings — a bleak structure for a bleak location. *Lens of Sutton collection*

Left: Equally bleak and desolate was Stoke Junction Halt, the last stop before the line to Grain and Port Victoria diverged from that to All Hallows-on-Sea. The photograph was taken *c*1960. *Author's collection*

Below: A 'C'-class 0-6-0 approaches Stoke Junction with the 11.50am Grain–Gravesend Central service on 24 October 1953. *Lens of Sutton collection*

Right: Grain Crossing Halt *c*1951, by which time a more substantial structure was being built to serve the new oil refinery, visible on the left. *Lens of Sutton collection*

Below: The newly completed Grain station, with its long central island platform, electric lighting and modern brick-built signalbox, pictured on 9 July 1955. A Brighton pull-push set, No 757, stands at the platform, ready for those refinery workers who had not yet purchased cars. The station would last only 10 years, closing on 1 December 1961. *J. H. Aston*

Right: Port Victoria pier station *c*1901, with a 'Q'-class 0-4-4T and a train of ex-LCDR six-wheel stock waiting to depart. Port Victoria was an important station at this time, with a connecting steam-packet service to Flushing; it was also used by the Royal Family for official (and not so official) journeys to the Continent. *Lens of Sutton collection*

Right: View of Port Victoria *c*1925, after the trains ceased running up the pier, showing the shortened section of line at the landward end. The station building was still in use as offices at this time. The pier would eventually be shortened further, due to marine-worm infestation. *Author's collection*

Above: Port Victoria in its final incarnation, cut right back to the land side, on 17 October 1948, with 'R1' 0-4-4T No 1665 awaiting the 'right away' at the head of a Brighton pull-push set forming a service to Gravesend Central. In the background can be seen the rotten remains of the pier, largely demolished in 1940 on account of being a hazard to navigation. The station was to close on 10 June 1951, when the new station at Grain opened. *W. A. Camwell / R. M. Casserley collection*

Right: The original station at All Hallows-on-Sea shortly after opening on 14 May 1932, as the terminus of a single-track branch from Middle Stoke. This view shows the contractors tidying up, while on the right, in store under a tarpaulin, is the Manning Wardle 0-6-0ST used in the construction work. *Lens of Sutton collection*

Right: The new seaside resort was at first well received by Londoners who wished to take a day trip out of their urban environment, and it was necessary to rebuild the terminus as an island platform and double the line from Middle Stoke to All Hallows-on-Sea. However, this situation changed postwar with the changed holiday habits of Londoners, who, with more money to spend, were off to pastures new, and the All Hallows-on-Sea branch withered. The photograph shows the rebuilt station *c*1946. *Lens of Sutton collection*

Right: A quiet afternoon at All Hallows-on-Sea, with 'H'-class 0-4-4T No 31517 waiting to depart for Gravesend Central. *Author's collection*

Below: After an exciting rainy afternoon *c*1955 at All Hallows-on-Sea it is time to head for home past the (closed) café advertising minerals and ices and onto the draughty platform for the train to Gravesend Central. 'See you all next year.' *R. K. Blencowe collection*

THE NEW ROMNEY and DUNGENESS BRANCHES

We have looked already at some remote and desolate locations for branch lines in north Kent along the Thames Estuary, but the New Romney and Dungeness branches served an area of equal desolation comprising flat reclaimed land with a high population of sheep interspersed with a few villages and medium-sized market towns. So what, aside from the livestock traffic, would prompt a major railway company to build a line through such a remote region? The answer stems from the bitter rivalry between two very powerful and determined self-made men — Sir Edward Watkin of the South Eastern Railway and James Staats-Forbes of the London, Chatham & Dover — who shared a mutual distaste and would stop at nothing to outdo one another.

The first move towards building a line in this area was projected in July 1866 as the New Romney Railway, intended to provide a link with the Hastings–Ashford main line at Appledore, but the powers to build the line were allowed to lapse.

By the early 1870s a fresh look was being taken at the area with a view to developing Dungeness as a major port with a faster cross-Channel journey time allowing an earlier arrival in Paris than was possible when travelling via Dover or Folkestone. In 1873 the Rye & Dungeness Railway & Pier Co was established to construct the line to Dungeness. However, this line was not constructed, and by 1875 the powers had passed to the South Eastern Railway. By the end of the 1870s Sir Edward Watkin had started to take an interest in this venture, to the extent that extensive research and planning went ahead with a view to providing a link between Dungeness and the French fishing port of Tréport, 114 miles from Paris.

With all this in the planning stage the Lydd Railway Co was formed on 8 April 1881 and was authorised to construct a single-track line from Appledore to Lydd via Brookland. Like a great number of railways at this time this company was on paper an independent concern. However, it very soon became part of the SER, the Chairman during its independent days being Alfred Mellor Watkin, son of Sir Edward. The engineer in charge of constructing the line was Francis Brady, and the contractor was T. A. Walker. The branch opened on 7 December 1881 for passenger traffic to Lydd and goods to Dungeness. On 24 July 1882 the company was authorised to build an extension from Lydd to New Romney and a northern extension from Appledore to Headcorn via Tenterden. A further authorisation, on 25 January 1883, allowed the company to build a line from Headcorn to Loose, near Maidstone. The line between Lydd and New Romney opened to all traffic on 19 June 1884, but the other two extensions were not pursued. In January 1885 the Lydd Railway was absorbed by the SER, which from the start had provided it with locomotives and rolling stock.

The great port at Dungeness would never be built, and the high hopes and expectations of the line's promoters came to nothing. However, in the case of the New Romney branch things took a different turn with developments in the early decades of the 20th century.

Left: Bathed in spring sunshine, Appledore station enjoys a moment of quiet between trains on 25 April 1947. This was the junction for the Dungeness and New Romney branches, the photograph being taken in the direction of Ashford. Note the 'C'-class 0-6-0 in front of the goods shed (left). *H. C. Casserley*

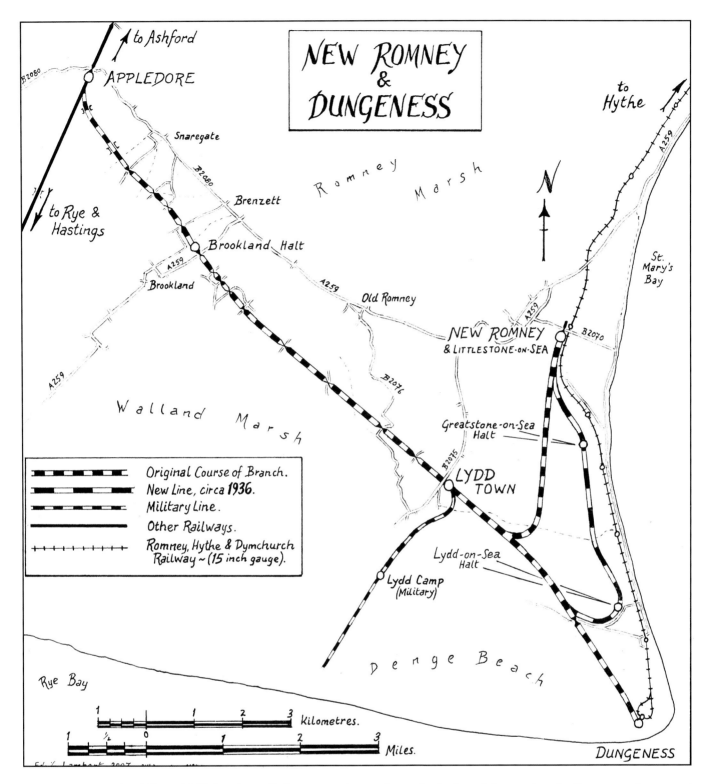

NEW ROMNEY & DUNGENESS

to Ashford

APPLEDORE

to Rye & Hastings

Snaregate

Brenzett

Brookland Halt

Brookland

Walland Marsh

Rye Bay

Romney Marsh

Old Romney

to Hythe

St. Mary's Bay

NEW ROMNEY
& LITTLESTONE-ON-SEA

Greatstone-on-Sea Halt

LYDD TOWN

Lydd-on-Sea Halt

Lydd Camp
(Military)

Denge Beach

DUNGENESS

Legend:
- Original Course of Branch.
- New Line, circa **1936**.
- Military Line.
- Other Railways.
- Romney, Hythe & Dymchurch Railway ~ (15 inch gauge).

Kilometres.

Miles.

In 1899 the warring SER and LCDR at last called a truce and formed a joint management committee, and during the period 1900-22 the line to New Romney settled down to become a backwater serving the local community, transporting farm produce and livestock (mostly sheep) to market. However, during the Great War the section between Lydd and New Romney, running along the Channel coast, was open to attack, and at Lydd the Royal Artillery had a rail connection to a firing range, which was to remain in use until the 1950s.

In 1923 the South Eastern & Chatham Railway Joint Committee became part of the newly formed Southern Railway. Within a few years the opening of holiday camps along the coast and the construction of the Romney, Hythe & Dymchurch Light Railway had changed a sleepy backwater of a branch line into a vibrant enterprise with some sort of future, the Southern Railway deciding

to invest in the branch by moving the line nearer the sea and constructing two new halts to serve the holiday-camp traffic. The new stations were at Greatstone-on-Sea and Lydd-on-Sea, the original station at Lydd being renamed Lydd Town, and the new alignment joined the Dungeness branch at a location that became known as Romney Junction. All of this was opened on 4 June 1937, following which the original line between Lydd and New Romney was closed.

The branch took on a new importance during World War 2, when, along with the RHDR, it found itself in the front line after the fall of France in 1940. It was during this period, on 26 November 1943, that Brighton 'D3' 0-4-4 tank No 2365 was attacked while heading a passenger train north of Lydd. The German FW190 aircraft crashed nearby; it is thought that the upsurge of steam from the damaged locomotive dome distracted the pilot, who was flung out of the aircraft and drowned in a nearby dyke. Happily the locomotive crew were unharmed and returned to duties, while the locomotive itself was soon repaired, re-boilered and returned to the branch.

After the war the line returned to its normal pace of life, transporting holidaymakers, livestock and local farm produce. In 1946, however, it was used for the filming of *The Loves of Joanna Godden*, set in Romney Marsh and starring Googie Withers in the leading role. The film company hired Kent & East Sussex locomotive No 3 and had also wanted to borrow derelict ex-LSWR six-wheeled carriages from the KESR, but the Southern Railway would not have them on its metals, so South Eastern & Chatham non-corridor bogie stock had to suffice. It is strange how film producers have such out-of-context notions, No 3 — a one-time Brighton locomotive — being re-lettered 'SECR', as though the Southern had no appropriate locomotives to lend!

On 1 January 1948 the line changed hands for the fourth time when it became part of British Railways' Southern Region. During the 1950s things settled down to a steady pace with branch services in the winter centred on Appledore, the pick-up goods serving all stations along the branch. In the summer there was additional excursion traffic from London, bringing the campers and day-trippers to enjoy the local delights and the Romney, Hythe & Dymchurch line along the coast. By contrast the section of line from Romney Junction to Dungeness (which had closed to passengers on 4 June 1937) closed to goods traffic in May 1953. This annual pattern of traffic continued until the early 1960s, when under the Beeching Plan, it was decided to close the line to passengers — this despite the holiday traffic, which continued to be lucrative. Goods services to/from New Romney ceased during 1964, and the passenger service followed suit on 6 March 1967. This left just the goods service to Lydd Town, which continued until 4 October 1971, and the nuclear-flask traffic to the siding at Dungeness Power Station (opened in the mid-1950s), which today is the only service over the branch.

Over the years the branch saw a variety of locomotives, starting with the SER Cudworth 2-4-0 tender locomotives and standard 0-6-0 goods, which were followed by Stirling 'A', 'B' and 'F' 4-4-0 passenger types and also 'O', 'O1' and 'C' 0-6-0 goods locomotives. Later Kitson steam railcars and 'H'-class 0-4-4 tanks were extensively used. After 1899 LCDR 'K'-class 4-4-0s, 'H'-class 0-6-0s and 'R'-class 0-4-4 tanks were also employed.

In Southern Railway days various Brighton tanks ran on the line, including 'D3' 0-4-4Ts and 'E4' 0-6-2Ts, while under British Railways it gained more-modern motive power in the form of Ivatt 2-6-2 tanks and BR Derby Type 2 (Class 24) Bo-Bo diesels, of which 15 were loaned to the Southern Region from 1958 pending the arrival of the BRCW Type 3 'Cromptons' (Class 33), which would also appear on the branch. In the last years 'Hampshire' diesel units of two- and three-car formations were used, although 'Hastings' units occasionally worked excursions over the line.

Carriage stock included various SER and SECR corridor and non-corridor four- and six-wheelers and bogie types, later replaced with Southern Maunsell and Bulleid designs. Also used on the line before and immediately after World War 2 were ex-LBSCR Billinton motor-fitted sets, while the early 1960s witnessed the arrival of BR Mk 1 stock, hauled by BR and BRCW diesel locomotives.

Below left: Ex-LBSCR 'D3' 0-4-4T No 2388 arrives at Appledore on 25 April 1947 with the 10.45am service from New Romney to Ashford. *H. C. Casserley*

Right: Brookland station *c*1910, viewed in the direction of Appledore. At this time the station had a passing-loop, which would be removed in BR days. *Lens of Sutton collection*

Below: Photograph of Brookland station taken in the direction of Appledore on 20 June 1958, by which date the passing-loop had been removed. *H. C. Casserley*

Bottom: Lydd Town station on 19 November 1966, only four months before closure to passengers (on 6 March 1967). It remained open to goods traffic until 4 October 1971. *R. K. Blencowe*

Left: 'F1' 4-4-0 No 140 arrives at Lydd with a goods train for Appledore on 17 October 1929. *H. C. Casserley*

Below left: A scene from the Great War, with troops arriving at Lydd for training at the Royal Artillery camp *c*1915. An 'O1' 0-6-0 runs round the troop train it has brought into the station. *Author's collection*

Above: A rare photograph of Lydd Camp *c*1890, showing the internal railway with mixed-gauge track and the bell tents pitched for the summer camp. *E. Carpenter collection*

Left: The station at Dungeness, serving the lighthouse and radio station, had very basic facilities, being used here *c*1930 by passengers awaiting the next train. Later the Romney, Hythe & Dymchurch Railway would also build a station here. *Lens of Sutton collection*

Top: 'O1'-class No 370 arrives at Dungeness on 5 September 1930 with an excursion train composed of ex-SECR 'birdcage' stock. *Pamlin Prints*

Above: With the re-routing of the New Romney branch, which reopened on 4 June 1937, two new halts were opened, at Lydd-on-Sea and Greatstone-on-Sea. In this photograph, taken c1961 an Ivatt 2-6-2T arrives at the former with a set of three Maunsell bogie carriages bound for New Romney. *Lens of Sutton collection*

Right: An empty platform at Greatstone-on-Sea Halt in the summer of 1961. *Author's collection*

Above: A quiet moment at New Romney & Littlestone-on-Sea, 17 October 1929. 'H'-class 0-4-4T No 162 stands at the platform with a train for Appledore as the driver oils the locomotive's inside motion and the guard chats with some locals by the station shelter. *H. C. Casserley*

Left: 'R1' 0-4-4T No 1663 and a Brighton pull-push set wait to depart New Romney for Appledore *c*1936. *Lens of Sutton collection*

Below: 'F1'-class 4-4-0 No 1151 at New Romney on 14 June 1936, having arrived from Appledore with a train of two ex-SECR non-corridor bogie carriages. *S. W. Baker*

Right: View of New Romney station from the roadside *c*1959, showing the booking office and main entrance.
Author's collection

Below: In the last years of the line's operation three-car 'Hampshire' diesel units were used. Here a unit in green livery with a small yellow panel waits at New Romney on a local service on 19 November 1966.
R. K. Blencowe collection

Bottom: The opposite end of the same train, viewed from the buffer stops at New Romney. Within four months this station would close, New Romney thereafter being served only by the Romney, Hythe & Dymchurch Railway.
R. K. Blencowe collection

The Romney, Hythe & Dymchurch Railway

After the Great War Britain's working population started to take a week's annual holiday, the Kent coast becoming a favourite destination, and it was this that prompted Capt J. E. P. Howey and his friend Count Zborowski, with the help of engineer Henry Greenly, to design the 15in-gauge Romney, Hythe & Dymchurch Railway, which opened in July 1927. An extension south from New Romney to Dungeness was opened in 1929, extending the line to a length of 13½ miles overall.

This miniature main line, which was initially double-tracked throughout, was a marvel of its time with its Henry Greenly-designed locomotive and bogie carriage stock running along the coast at relatively high speeds for a narrow-gauge line. It is hard to believe also that during World War 2 the RHDR, by now in the 'front line', operated armoured trains hauled by a Greenly 2-8-2 locomotive and comprising converted bogie ballast hoppers upon which were mounted Lewis and Bren guns.

The Southern Railway and, later, BR Southern Region always gave the line support as it generated considerable traffic for the New Romney branch right up until the latter's closure to passengers in the 1960s, and happily the RHDR survives today as an important tourist attraction in this part of Kent.

Above: The first locomotive to run on the RHDR was a German-built Krauss 0-4-0 tender/tank engine, *The Bug*, built in 1926. This was used for constructing the 15in-gauge railway but found little use on the line after it opened in 1927. In 1935 *The Bug* was sold to a miniature railway at Belle View Park in Belfast, where it was renamed *Jean*. It was sold from there to a scrap dealer in Northern Ireland, from where it was rescued by Bill McAlpine and restored to working order for the RHDR, where it is occasionally used on specials. *Ian Allan Library*

Above right: Hythe station on 27 July 1947 with Greenley Pacific No 2 *Northern Chief* and Canadian-type Pacific No 9 *Winston Churchill* awaiting departure. *J. C. Flemons*

Below right: Canadian-type Pacific No 10 *Dr Syn* leaves Dymchurch with a train for New Romney on 27 July 1947. The RHDR had made a great recovery after World War 2, as is apparent from the photograph, although by now the line south from New Romney had been singled. *J. C. Flemons*

Below: One of the Greenly Pacifics, No 2 *Northern Chief,* at Hythe in the early 1930s with a train of the original articulated carriage stock on a New Romney service. *Ian Allan Library*

Above: RHDR locomotives frequently visited other railways. Here Greenly Pacific No 1 *Green Goddess* is unloaded from a Southern machinery truck onto the 15in-gauge Ravenglass & Eskdale Railway at Ravenglass for an exchange visit in the early 1930s. *M. J. Fair*

Right: The designer and his creation. Henry Greenly points with his cane to a detail on the trailing axlebox on No 1 *Green Goddess* at New Romney shed *c*1927. *Ian Allan Library*

Above left: Passing trains between Hythe and New Romney as two Greenly Pacifics meet halfway through their journeys. No 3 *Southern Maid* speeds by with a fast service to Hythe on 23 July 1947. *J. C. Flemons*

Left: On the same day No 1 *Green Goddess* leaves Dungeness for Hythe with the 'Blue Coaster Limited' — one of many named trains to run on the RHDR over the years. Note the new Ashford Works-built tender behind the locomotive. *J. C. Flemons*

Right: Laurel and Hardy share a joke with driver Monty Baker during their visit to the RHDR in 1947. *Ian Allan Library*

THE CANTERBURY & WHITSTABLE RAILWAY

The railways examined thus far have all been products of the mid-/late 19th century or the early years of the 20th century. By contrast the Canterbury & Whitstable Railway was far more important in terms of railway history, being the first steam-operated line built and opened in the South East of England — in 1830, the same year as the Liverpool & Manchester Railway, the world's first inter-city line.

In 1823 railway pioneer William James, recognising that transport problems were thwarting the area's potential, suggested to Canterbury City Council that a line from the city to the Thames Estuary at Whitstable would be of great benefit to commerce in east Kent. Several routes were surveyed which were eventually narrowed down to one, authorised on 10 June 1825, in the same year that the Stockton & Darlington Railway, the world's first public steam railway, opened.

Engineer to the line was none other than George Stephenson, John Dixon of Darlington being appointed Resident Engineer, while the contract to lay the track was awarded to Joseph Locke,

who had been trained by Stephenson. However, in the early years of construction the project experienced financial difficulties, such that work came to a standstill shortly after the completion of Tyler Hill Tunnel in 1827. By the time of re-financing John Dixon had left the company, being replaced by Robert Stephenson, who then appointed Joshua Richardson as Resident Engineer.

The line had some steep gradients and in its early days was partially cable-worked by two stationary engines, at the top of Tyler Hill and at Clowes Wood, to which was later added a third, at Bogshole. The company also possessed a steam locomotive, *Invicta*, used primarily at the Whitstable end of the line for hauling trains from the harbour to the site of the first stationary engine, where it gave way to cable working. Designed by Stephenson, it was built at the same time as the *Rocket*, but the latter had the benefit of a Booth water-tube boiler. By contrast *Invicta* was not a total success and was withdrawn and put into store in 1839, having been replaced by four strong horses. Fortunately this early example of locomotive engineering was later preserved by the

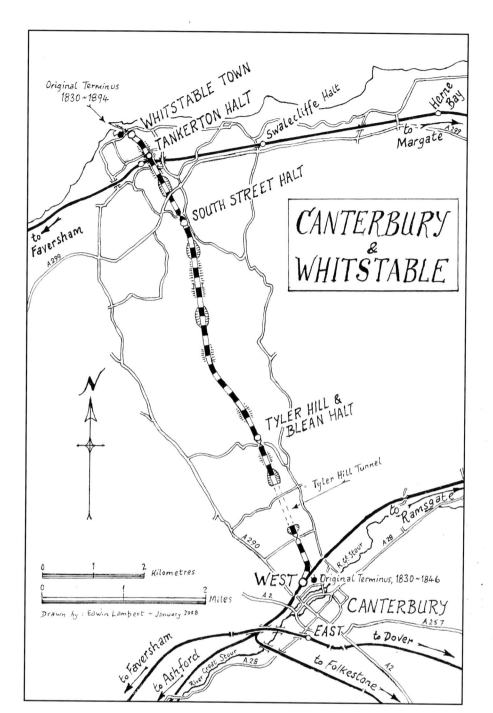

Below left: The only tangible relic of the Canterbury & Whitstable Railway today is the Stephenson-designed 0-4-0 locomotive *Invicta*, built for £635 in 1829, which is now thankfully on display under cover in Canterbury Museum after spending many decades out in all weathers in Dane John Gardens in Canterbury, as seen here on 23 May 1959. *R. C. Riley*

Below: Canterbury West station main entrance c1959. This was the second station, which replaced the building constructed when the South Eastern Railway opened is main line in the 1840s. *Author's collection*

South Eastern Railway, which presented it to Canterbury City Council, and it can nowadays be seen in Canterbury Museum.

Established at the dawn of the railway era, the Canterbury & Whitstable was somewhat primitive, to say the least. There were no proper station buildings along the line, and at Whitstable Harbour the station consisted of a basic platform upon which stood a timber hut. The train service, meanwhile, had no timetable, and passengers travelled in open wagons with only covers, supported by four stanchions, affording protection from the elements. To improve the situation the company was later forced to purchase some proper carriage stock, funded by an increase in fares. Despite this the operation of the line in early days was somewhat lax, cable haulage being used on the way up to Whitstable and gravity on the way down, which led to some very nasty accidents.

By 1838 the company had got into financial difficulties, to the extent that it was forced to offer the line for lease. Operation passed to Nicholson & Bayless, but in 1841 this company went bankrupt, leaving the Canterbury & Whitstable in need of another to operate the line. Eventually, in 1844, the South Eastern Railway took over the lease, following which things began to change for the better.

Among the earliest improvements were those to stations, as well as a complete re-laying of the track. With the heavier track in place the South Eastern Railway started using conventional steam locomotives and rolling stock in 1846. The new leaseholder also started to improve the harbour at Whitstable, while the line's original southern terminus in Canterbury was closed, trains being diverted to the SER's station via its Canterbury–Ramsgate line; the original station at Canterbury was, however, retained for goods traffic.

Facilities at Whitstable Harbour station were further improved in 1894, when the old station was closed and replaced by a new station on the opposite side of Harbour Street. In 1899, following the formation of the South Eastern & Chatham Railway Companies' Joint Management Committee, a spur was laid to link the branch with the London, Chatham & Dover Railway's Faversham–Margate line. In 1908 a new halt was opened at Tyler Hill, and on 1 June 1911 a similar halt was opened at South Street. A third halt was opened at Tankerton in July 1914.

The first SER locomotives that could be used on the line were the '119'-class Tayleur 0-6-0s. This was because of the restricted bore of Tyler Hill Tunnel, which was to remain a problem throughout the line's existence, as all locomotives used thereon had to have cabs, domes and chimneys of reduced height. Other types used were the South Eastern 'R'-class 0-6-0 tanks and 'O1' 0-6-0s. From 1890 the 'R'-class 0-6-0Ts (rebuilt as 'R1s' from 1910) were the normal motive power, remaining thus until closure.

On 1 January 1923 the line became part of the Southern Railway, which maintained the *status quo* until the late 1920s, when it became apparent that receipts were declining, largely as a result of road competition, and the passenger service was duly withdrawn with effect from 2 January 1931.

Goods continued until after nationalisation on 1 January 1948, by which time the service had been reduced to just one return working each weekday. Whitstable Harbour having fallen into disuse, the decision was taken to withdraw goods services with effect from 1 December 1952. The line had a short reprieve after the serious floods of early 1953, being used to convey materials for 23 days from 5 February, after which it closed to all traffic.

Left: 'R1'-class 0-6-0T No 147 and a train of ex-LCDR six-wheel stock at the Canterbury & Whitstable platform at Canterbury West *c*1930, awaiting the signal to start its journey to Whitstable. This was not the location of the original Canterbury & Whitstable station, which was about a mile to the east. *Author's collection*

Left: 'R1' 0-6-0T No 31339, fitted with a Bulleid cut-down stovepipe chimney, runs into the bay platform at Canterbury West in the summer of 1952 with a train of open mineral wagons from Whitstable. *P. Ransome-Wallis*

Right: Hanover Arch, Canterbury, *c*1952, with its footpath under the branch to Whitstable. *J. W. Sparrowe*

Below: The way ahead on a June day in 1950 as 'R1' 0-6-0T No 31339 heads past the remains of Tyler Hill Halt with a goods train from Whitstable to Canterbury. *P. Ransome-Wallis*

Right: Heading for Canterbury West, an 'R'-class 0-6-0T in original condition drops down the bank from Tyler Hill Halt *c*1898 with a mixed train consisting of four- and six-wheel carriages, a string of open wagons and a brake van. *Author's collection*

Left: An 'R'-class 0-6-0T in original condition runs out of Tyler Hill Tunnel *c*1898 with a goods train for Canterbury West comprising tarpaulin-covered open wagons and a brake van. *Ian Allan Library*

Right: Forty-one years later 'R1' 0-6-0T No 1147 descends the same bank with a similar train of tarpaulin-covered wagons bound for Canterbury West. *Roger Carpenter*

Left: Emerging from the tight confines of Tyler Hill Tunnel, 'R1' 0-6-0T No 31010 heads south with a goods train in the summer of 1952. *P. Ransome-Wallis*

Right: 'R1' 0-6-0T No 31070 blasts out of the north portal of Tyler Hill Tunnel on its way to Whitstable with a goods train on 3 September 1952. The normal operation of the 'R1' 0-6-0Ts on this line was with the bunker facing towards Whitstable and smokebox towards Canterbury West. *P. Winding*

Below: View of South Street Halt, Whitstable, shortly before closure in 1931, showing the platform, level crossing and the basic station buildings. *Roger Carpenter*

Bottom: Creating a spectacular photograph, 'King Arthur' 4-6-0 No 796 *Sir Dodinas Le Savage* speeds past with a Victoria–Ramsgate express as 'R1' 0-6-0T No 31069 poses on the bridge near Whitstable in the summer of 1946. *P. Ransome-Wallis*

Left: With a cloud of thick black smoke issuing from its squat chimney, 'R'-class 0-6-0T No 124 waits to depart Whitstable for Canterbury West *c*1925 This was the second station at Whitstable, opened after the SER had taken over the Canterbury & Whitstable Railway in 1844. The mixed train is of interest, consisting of four ex-LCDR four-wheel carriages and a string of tarpaulin-covered open wagons. *H. C. Casserley*

Above: Whitstable station after closure, devoid of life and with all its signals removed. The photograph dates from *c*1932. *J. W. Sparrowe*

Left: A last look at the branch's passenger service, with 'R'-class 0-6-0T No 126 and a mixed train of ex-LCDR four-wheel stock and open wagons about to begin the journey from Whitstable to Canterbury West *c*1928. *M. D. England*

Above: A general view of Whitstable Harbour c1930. In the foreground is the original station, which had not seen passengers since the mid-19th century. *J. W. Sparrowe*

Left: The original Whitstable Harbour station as at Easter 1939, with 'R1' 0-6-0T No 1147 shunting the harbour sidings before marshalling a train and returning to Canterbury West later in the day. *Roger Carpenter*

Below: A Thames barge loads a cargo at the quayside as the Southern Railway four-wheel steam crane stands on the siding along the top of the quay. These is much activity as a lorry is being unloaded in the background. *J. W. Sparrowe*

THE FOLKESTONE HARBOUR BRANCH

The Folkestone Harbour branch was quite unlike the other lines covered in this book in that it was built as an extension of the main line from London to the Kent Coast to tap the cross-Channel traffic to the Continent. Although the ports at both Dover and Folkestone catered for this important traffic there were restrictions at Dover in operational terms because the harbour was actually owned by the Dover Harbour Company, which understandably put its own interests before those of the South Eastern or London, Chatham & Dover railways.

The South Eastern Railway took an early interest in Folkestone Harbour, which dated back to 1809 but by the 1840s had become derelict. Having built its main line from London to the Kent coast, the SER took over Folkestone Harbour and in 1843, to serve the newly instituted cross-Channel ferry service, constructed a double-track branch from what became known as Folkestone

Junction. The branch included a section on brick viaduct, as well as a lattice-girder swing bridge to allow shipping into the inner harbour. Thereafter Folkestone became the main hub for Continental shipping, remaining thus until the 1890s (by which time Dover, where the Admiralty had built a pier in the middle of the 19th century, had caught up with it as an important harbour with modern facilities), although for its first six years the Folkestone Harbour branch was a goods-only line.

In 1905 further extensions were made at Folkestone Harbour to improve the facilities that had helped to revive its fortunes. The outbreak of war in August 1914 changed the situation for both Dover and Folkestone. Dover Marine station opened in 1915, further improving facilities at that port, which at that time, like Folkestone, was used almost exclusively for military traffic in support of the war effort. This continued until 1918,

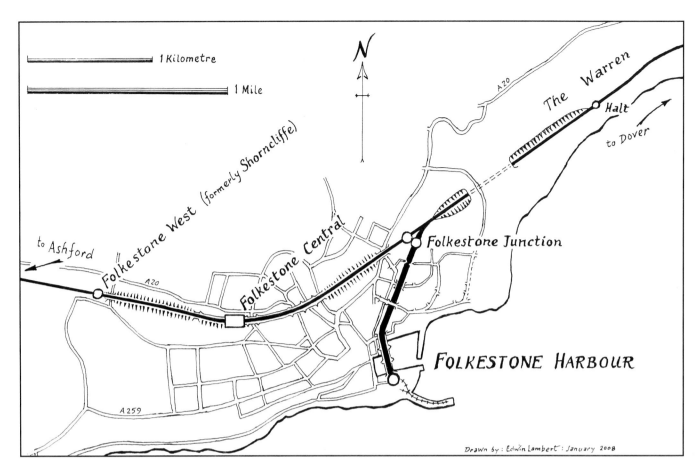

Drawn by: Edwin Lambert: January 2008

and it was not until the following year that Continental traffic returned.

During the 1920s and '30s traffic improved with more people wishing to visit Paris and the Continent. The introduction in the mid-1930s of the 'Golden Arrow' and the 'Night Ferry' further increased traffic until the outbreak of World War 2 in September 1939. During the war Dover and Folkestone reverted to military use, which continued until the end of hostilities in 1945. During this period both ports played an important role in the war, notably in Operation 'Dynamo' during the evacuation of the British Expeditionary Force from the beaches of Dunkirk and assisting in the defence of the South Coast.

After the war things returned to normal with the resumption of cross-Channel traffic as well as normal train services. These were steam-hauled; although, before the war, the Southern Railway had planned the electrification of main and secondary lines, it was left to British Railways to carry out this plan after 1948. By the late 1950s the network from London to the Kent coast was in the process of being electrified, spelling the end of steam traction in Kent other than in a number of small enclaves. In February 1962 the power signalbox at Folkestone Junction replaced the mechanical 'boxes in the area, and on 18 June electrification of passenger services was completed, although the majority, including the prestigious 'Golden Arrow', had been converted in June 1961.

Left: Line-up of Wainwright locomotives at Folkestone Junction shed on 31 October 1937. On the left is an unidentified 'P'-class 0-6-0T, behind which is an 'R1' with an original Stirling cab, while on the right are 'R1' 0-6-0Ts Nos 1107 and 1174. Folkestone Junction was the depot that provided the motive power for the Folkestone Harbour branch up until 1961, when steam traction ceased in this part of Kent.
R. M. Casserley collection

Right: A trio of 'R1' 0-6-0Ts, No 31069 leading, crest the bank at Folkestone Junction c1955 with a boat train for London Victoria.
R. K. Blencowe collection

Further changes took place in August 1968 with the closure of the harbour sidings to goods traffic, but probably the greatest upheaval came with the construction of the Channel Tunnel and the consequent decline of Folkestone as a port. Dover Marine station closed following the opening of the tunnel in 1994, and the Folkestone Harbour branch now saw only two trains a day, from London Charing Cross, to connect with the 11.15 and 13.15 'Sea Cat' sailings to Boulogne. Following the transfer of the 'Sea Cats' to Ramsgate these regular services ceased, following which only occasional use was made of the branch.

In May 2002 Train Protection & Warning System was installed, but the up line was lifted. In 2006 it was announced that there were plans to redevelop the harbour as a marina and to demolish the railway viaduct. The last VSOE Pullman ran in November 2006, and 12 April 2008 saw the running of what was officially the last train to use the branch. In the next few years the line will probably be closed, bringing to an end a long and colourful chapter in the history of Kent's railways.

Locomotive types used for most of the branch's existence were Stirling 'R'-class 0-6-0 tanks and, later, the rebuilt 'R1' versions, as well as the Wainwright 'P'-class 0-6-0Ts, which were used as dock shunters at the port. In the late 1950s, by which time the 'R1s' were getting long in the tooth, the Southern Region borrowed some ex-Great Western 0-6-0 pannier tanks of the '57xx' class, and it was these locomotives that were to see out steam traction on the harbour branch in the period leading up to electrification in 1961.

Left: Three 'R1s', Nos 31107, 31047 and 31154, head for Folkestone Junction with Bulleid stock forming a boat train to London Victoria on 17 August 1954. *R. K. Blencowe collection*

Below: Assisted by a sister locomotive at the rear, 'R'-class 0-6-0T No 342 powers up the bank with a seven-carriage boat train *c*1925. The first four carriages are ex-SECR matchboard bogie stock. *Author's collection*

Above: An early pen-and-ink drawing of the original swing-bridge across the harbour at Folkestone *c*1850, showing the harbour as reconstructed by the South Eastern Railway. *Ian Allan Library*

Below: A photograph of the same swing- bridge on 14 May 1927, with 'R'-class 0-6-0T No 153 about to cross the structure while running light-engine. *H. C. Casserley*

Above: 'R1' 0-6-0T No 31337 at Folkestone Ferry Terminal on 19 May 1957, having arrived with a Stephenson Locomotive Society special. *H. C. Casserley*

Right: Manning Wardle 0-6-0ST No 353, which prior to the Great War served for many years as the SECR's harbour shunter at Folkestone. *Author's collection*

Above Left: 'R1' 0-6-0T No 31128 leaves Folkestone Harbour with the empty stock of the 'Golden Arrow' on 14 August 1959. *R. M. Casserley*

Left: An aerial view of Folkestone Harbour *c*1956, with an 'R1' 0-6-0T heading a boat train across the viaduct towards the junction. Beyound the train can be seen the outer harbour and its breakwater, while in the foreground small boats are moored on the still waters of the inner harbour. *R. K. Blencowe*

Right: 'P'-class 0-6-0T No A27 shunts the Ferry Quay on 14 May 1927. The locomotive is coupled to a container flat, which is being loaded by a harbour crane. *H. C. Casserley*

THE HYTHE & SANDGATE BRANCH

When the South Eastern Railway built its main line to Folkestone in the 1840s, Hythe was by-passed on account of the need to take a level route. This was despite the fact that Hythe was then considered more important than Folkestone, which prior to the construction of the SER's new harbour had become something a backwater. By contrast Hythe, aside from being a Cinque Port and having a military garrison, was at this time an important market town and an up-and-coming holiday resort.

Further along the coast from Hythe there was considerable development at Seabrook and Sandgate. By the early 1860s the three towns were becoming very popular, as a result of which the South Eastern Railway decided to build a branch from Sandling Junction to Hythe and Sandgate.

The line was promoted in 1864, but it was not until 27 January 1870 that the SER finally helped to form a company to build the line. The Hythe & Sandgate Railway Co would own the land, and the SER would provide the finance to build the railway. The engineer for the project was Francis Brady, the contractor Philip Stiff of Dover, although the SER eventually completed the project alone. The 3½ mile branch was opened as a double-track line on 9 October 1874. The train service originally ran from Westenhanger station.

In 1876 the SER obtained permission to extend the line along the coast from Sandgate to Folkestone, but these powers were never taken up. Had the line been built it would have overcome a serious problem which has always dogged the Folkestone Harbour branch, which was built with very steep inclines.

Sandling Junction station was opened in 1888 with four platforms — two on the main line from Ashford to Folkestone and two on the branch. The Hythe & Sandgate ran through some very attractive country, passing close to Saltwood Castle on the way to Hythe and continuing thence under the cliffs to Sandgate. There was a short tunnel near the junction at Sandling, known as Hythe Tunnel.

In addition to building the branch a further 4 miles of horse tramway from Sandgate Hill along the coast to Hythe was built and opened in 1891. It was later nearly sold to the National Electric Construction Co, which intended to build a new electric tramway from Hythe to Folkestone, but this project came to nothing. The horse tramway was closed during the Great War from 1914 to 1918 but surprisingly reopened in 1919, finally being closed in 1921 by the South Eastern & Chatham Railway.

After the Great War and the Grouping of the railways on 1 January 1923 things changed with the need for economies to be made, especially where unremunerative branch lines were concerned, and the Southern Railway decided to close the line between Hythe and Sandgate on 1 April 1931. The section from Sandling Junction continued to see passenger and goods trains until temporary closure during World War 2 in 1943; reopened in 1945, it closed for good on 3 December 1951.

During its existence the branch saw a variety of motive power, ranging from Cudworth '118'-class 2-4-0s and 0-6-0 standard goods locomotives in the early days to 'Q' and 'Q1' 0-4-4 tanks during the Edwardian era and the Great War. Goods and passenger services were also handled by 'O' and 'O1' 0-6-0 goods locomotives, supplemented at times by 'C'-class 0-6-0s. During the 1930s Brighton 'D3' 0-4-4Ts and 'D1' 0-4-2Ts could be found on the line, and latterly 'H'-class 0-4-4Ts were employed. Carriage stock ranged from four- and six-wheel non-corridor coaches used originally to SECR and LBSCR non-corridor bogie stock employed in later years.

Right: The branch train from Hythe waits in the platform at Sandling Junction as a fast passenger service headed by a Maunsell 4-4-0 runs through in the summer of 1950. *R. C. Riley*

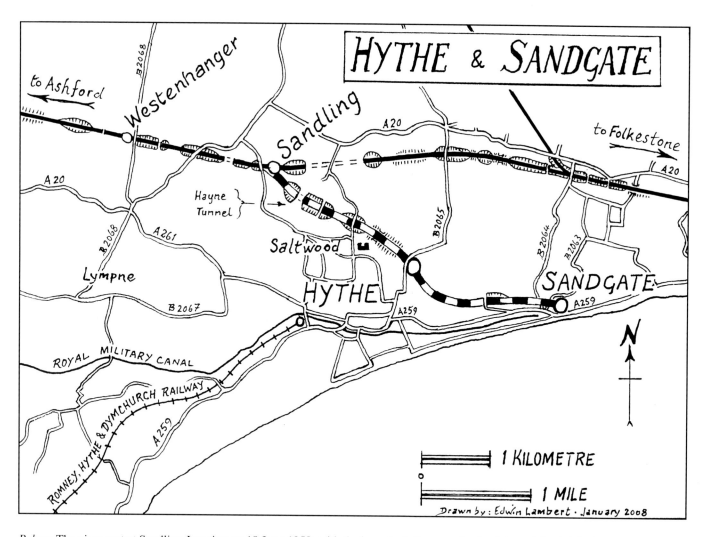

Below: The view east at Sandling Junction on 18 June 1958, with the branch platform on the far right and the Ashford–Folkestone line on the left. By this time the branch had closed to traffic, and the former branch platforms were being used for access to the station goods yard. *H. C. Casserley*

Above: Another view of Sandling Junction, on 18 June 1958, featuring the station building/ booking hall, which was detached from the main platforms. *H. C. Casserley*

Left: 'H'-class 0-4-4T No 31521 with its Brighton two-car pull-push set at Hythe in the summer of 1950. This photograph shows the two-platform station as it was just a year and a half before closure, which was effected on 3 December 1951. *R. C. Riley*

Below left: The same train viewed from the other platform, in the direction of Sandgate. *R. C. Riley*

Above right: Photograph of Hythe station taken *c*1935 in the direction of Sandling Junction, providing a good view of the station canopies. Just in shot on the left is the south signalbox.
Lens of Sutton collection

Right: Hythe station goods yard in the summer of 1950, with 'H'-class 0-4-4T No 31521 shunting between passenger turns. *R. C. Riley*

Left: 'O1' 0-6-0 No 385 heads for Sandgate with a train of LCDR and SER six-wheel and bogie stock near Saltwood on 17 June 1924. A year and a half after the Grouping, locomotive and rolling stock are still in late SECR livery. *F. J. Agar*

Below: An early view of Sandgate station, recorded *c*1880, with a train of SER four-wheel carriages waiting to depart for Sandling Junction behind a Cudworth 2-4-0. The photograph also shows well the development of this Victorian seaside town. *R. M. Casserley collection*

Bottom: Period postcard of the same scene *c*1890, featuring the station goods yard, with the town and beach beyond. *Lens of Sutton collection*

Seabrook in Sandgate

Above: Photograph of Sandgate station taken in September 1921 in the direction of Hythe and showing the second platform, often used for unloading goods wagons. *H. P. Rutherford*

Right: A Hythe & Sandgate horse tram ready to set off through the streets of Sandgate *c*1912. This horse-tram system, which was quite extensive, was owned by the South Eastern & Chatham Railway, which had purchased it from the original promoter with a view to selling it on to the National Electric Construction Co Ltd as part of the proposed Folkestone Tramway scheme. However, this did not come about, and although the tramway closed during the Great War it reopened in 1919, only to close for good in 1921. *Author's collection*

Right: A Hythe & Sandgate horse tram heading along the coast from Sandgate to Hythe *c*1910. *R. M. Casserley collection*

THE GRAVESEND WEST BRANCH

The Gravesend West branch was a further result of attempts by the rival South Eastern and London, Chatham & Dover railways to win valuable traffic from one another. The construction by the Thames & Medway Canal of a single-track railway along its towpath later led to the SER's purchasing the canal company and incorporating its route into the North Kent Line. The LCDR constructed its main line from London to Chatham five miles south of this line.

The proposal to build a branch from a junction to the west of Fawkham to Gravesend was first proposed in 1881 in order to tap into the valuable traffic to be found along the Thames Estuary which at that time was solely the preserve of the SER. The new branch was promoted as the Gravesend Railway Co, nominally an independent railway but heavily backed from the start by the LCDR.

Authorisation to build the line was passed on 18 July 1881. At this time the London, Tilbury & Southend Railway had proposed building a tunnel under the Thames for a line from their Tilbury terminus to Gravesend to link with the Gravesend West branch. Sadly this project came to nothing; had it come to fruition the whole railway history of the area would probably have been very different. The LTSR also intended to link with the SER North Kent line at Gravesend.

The engineer appointed to the project was C. D. Fox and the contractor was G. Barclay-Bruce. The branch ran from a junction to the west of Fawkham via Longfield, Southfleet and Rosherville before terminating at a pier on the Thames north of the SER station at Gravesend and was 5½ miles in length.

The original company was taken over by the LCDR on 29 June 1883, which also coincided with William Hill taking over as Chief Engineer from C. D. Fox. The branch opened to goods traffic on 17 April 1886, which was also the day that Tilbury Docks opened. On 10 May 1886 the line was opened to passenger traffic.

In addition to Thames-side traffic the company had high hopes of the potential for river traffic and that resulting from the opening of the pleasure gardens near Gravesend. In 1899 when the rivalry between the two railways ceased as the South Eastern & Chatham Railway Joint Management Committee came into being the name of the former LCDR station was changed to Gravesend West Street, and the former SER station became Gravesend Central to avoid confusion.

From the earliest days of the branch there were services run from London to connect with steamer services from the pier to Southend, Clacton and Walton-on-the-Naze in Essex. More important was the steamer service operated from the pier to Rotterdam which was introduced in 1916 by the Dutch-owned Royal Batavia Line and continued until 1939.

In 1910 Rosherville Pleasure Gardens closed down, which had an adverse effect on the finances of the line. In 1913 pull-push services were introduced as an economy measure, and a halt was opened at Longfield. After the Grouping in 1923, the line declined further and took on a more local flavour and only occasional boat trains ran to the pier from London. During Southern Railway days all through services from London, with the exception of boat trains, ceased running.

The service to Rotterdam resumed after World War 2 but did not return to Gravesend Pier, operating instead from Tilbury, which was a further nail in the coffin for the branch. However, the General Steam Navigation Co did operate pleasure steamers from the pier in the 1950s. After nationalisation in 1948 the line largely operated a local service, along with a few boat specials to/from the pier. During this period the pier station at Gravesend was renamed Gravesend West.

Passenger services declined further until they were finally withdrawn on 3 August 1953. During 1959 the line was singled to

Left: 'C'-class 0-6-0 No 31713 prepares to run round its train at Farningham Road station prior to departing with the 3.59pm service to Gravesend West on 11 April 1953. Note the Bulleid electric unit awaiting the signal at the platform on the right. *R. C. Riley*

Right: The view east at Farningham Road on 21 May 1938, featuring the large water tower, with its substantial brick base, and the covered footbridge. *H. C. Casserley*

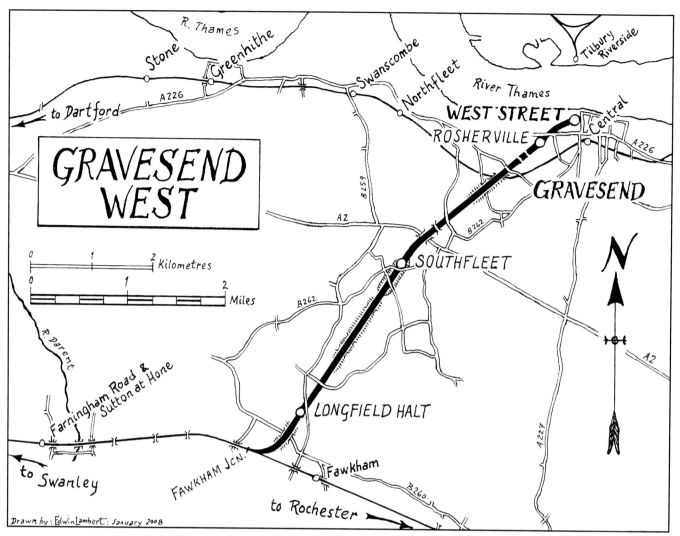

Drawn by: Edwin Lambert: January 2008

cut costs and the last goods train ran on 24 March 1968 after which the line was closed although the track was left in place for many years before being lifted. Today a stretch of the trackbed has returned to railway use, being used as the basis of part of the high-speed line to the Channel Tunnel.

It is hard to ascertain which classes of locomotive were used in the early period of the line's existence. They were probably LCDR 2-4-0Ts and 0-4-2WTs on local trains and a variety of 4-4-0 tender locomotives on boat trains. During SECR days 'R'- and, later, 'H'-class 0-4-4 tanks were used, supplemented during the Great War by 'P'-class 0-6-0 tanks. Boat trains were worked by a variety

of SECR 4-4-0s, and this pattern continued into Southern and British Railways days, when 'O'-, 'O1'- and 'C'-class 0-6-0s were used additionally on local goods trains and some boat-train services. Following the end of steam in Kent in June 1961, goods trains were entrusted to Class 33 diesel locomotives.

Carriage stock comprised a variety of four- and six-wheel non-corridor stock in LCDR and SECR days, although corridor and non-corridor bogie stock was employed on some local and boat-train services, and following the Grouping more-modern steel-panelled bogie stock started to appear on the line.

Left: 'R1'-class 0-4-4T No 31662 and pull-push motor set No 738 wait in the siding at Farningham Road between turns in the winter of 1953. *R. C. Riley*

Below left: Coupled to a Brighton pull-push motor set, 'R1' 0-4-4T No 1669 departs Farningham Road for Gravesend West on 21 May 1938. *H. C. Casserley*

Right: Bound for Farningham Road, 'C'-class 0-6-0 No 31713 arrives at Southfleet station on 11 April 1953 with a two-carriage train of ex-SECR bogie non-corridor stock. In the background (left) can be seen the station goods yard. *R. C. Riley*

Right: Pre-Grouping view of Rosherville station, recorded in the summer of 1921 and showing the station buildings and footbridge. The platforms are host to just one solitary lady passenger but have a fine collection of gas lamps. *Author's collection*

Below: Thirty-one years later, on 20 September 1952, an 'H'-class 0-4-4T and motor set depart Rosherville station on the 4.46 service for Farningham Road. *J. H. Aston*

Above: 'R1' 0-4-4T No 31662 makes a spirited departure from Gravesend West in the summer of 1952 with a motor set for Farningham Road. In the background a Maunsell 2-6-0 and a 'C'-class 0-6-0 simmer in the sidings with special trains awaiting passengers from Thames steamers. *K. W. Wightman*

Left: A panoramic view of Gravesend West station on 11 April 1953, showing the extensive track layout with its platform roads and goods facilities. 'C'-class 0-6-0 No 31723 shunts on the far right while the branch stock waits at the right-hand platform. *R. C. Riley*

Below: 'R1' 0-4-4T No 31662 blows off steam at Gravesend West on 18 July 1953 between turns from/to Farningham Road. Unusually the locomotive has arrived bunker-first. *R. C. Riley*

Above: On a bleak 10 January 1953, 'R1' No 31697 — still in Southern Railway postwar Bulleid livery — and its train of Brighton pull-push bogie stock await custom at Gravesend West. *H. C. Casserley*

Right: On 11 June 1938 'C'-class 0-6-0 No 1576 stands at the platform at Gravesend West Street (as the station was then known), having just arrived from London Victoria with the 6.30am boat train, consisting of an ex-SECR matchwood Brake Third (leading) and two Maunsell steel-bodied bogie composites. The Rotterdam steam-packet service with which this train connected would survive until the outbreak of World War 2. *H. C. Casserley*

Right: Gravesend West in the spring of 1953, this being the view towards the end of the pier and the Thames Estuary. Pull-push set No 657 stands next to a line of open wagons. *Lens of Sutton collection*

THE ELHAM VALLEY RAILWAY

The Elham Valley Railway Co was incorporated in 1864 to build a railway from Canterbury to Folkestone, thereby providing a direct route to this up-and-coming port, but nothing occurred until 1883, when] the London, Chatham & Dover Railway proposed building a line from Kearsney, on its Dover–Canterbury line.

The South Eastern Railway took a dim view of the LCDR's proposal and quickly reactivated the 1864 plan to ensure that its rival would not have easy access to Folkestone. In 1884 it took over the Elham Valley Railway Co, in order to build the blocking line and thereby maintain its hold on valuable traffic to Folkestone and its port. The railway, which ran from Cheriton Halt, on the Folkestone–Ashford main line, to a junction at Harbledown, on the Ashford–Ramsgate main line.

The line's engineer was Francis Brady, appointed by the South Eastern Railway, the contractor was T. A. Walker. The railway, which featured some impressive earthworks and heavy engineering, ran from Folkestone Central to Canterbury West via intermediate stations at Lyminge, Elham, Barham, Bishopsbourne, Bridge and Canterbury South. The line was opened on 4 July 1887 between Cheriton Junction and Barham, the remainder thence to Hambledown Junction, south of Canterbury, following suit on 1 July 1889.

For most of its existence the line had a sleepy feel about it, but during the Great War it was heavily used for military purposes. Indeed, soon after the outbreak of war a serious landslip near Martello Tunnel, Folkestone, effectively closed the direct line between there and Dover, as a result of which the Elham Valley line

LYMINGE STATION

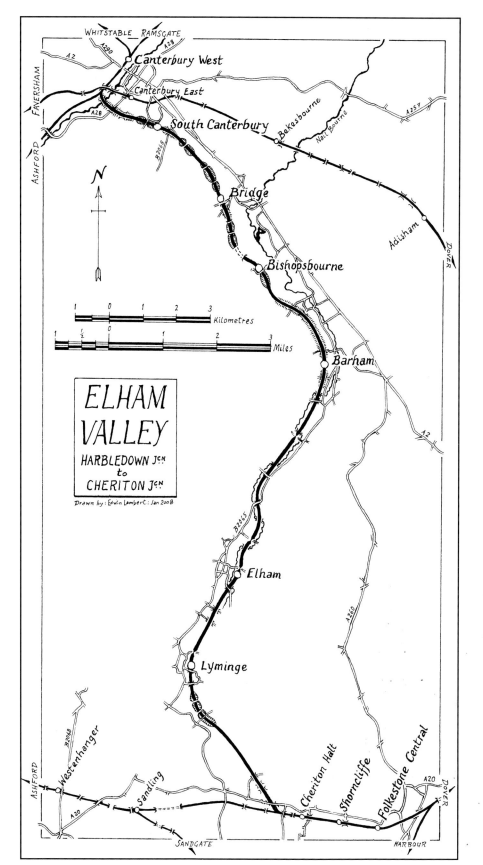

Left: A rare photograph of a train on the Elham Valley Railway, at Lyminge station *c*1924, comprising ex-SECR bogie stock headed by a 'Q'-class 0-4-4T. At this time the line was double-track and enjoyed through passenger and goods services from Folkestone Central to Canterbury East. *Lens of Sutton collection*

became the only rail link between the two ports (albeit by means a circuitous route via Canterbury) for most of the duration of the war. Despite this, and in common with many secondary lines at around this time, it was singled in 1916 as a temporary measure to provide track materials for the war effort, the second track being restored following the end of hostilities.

After the end of the war the East Kent Road Car Co introduced a local bus service which took away most of the passenger traffic.

As a result the Southern Railway decided to single the section between Canterbury and Lyminge in October 1931, leaving only the short section from Lyminge to Cheriton Junction as double track. However, both passenger and goods services continued until the outbreak of World War 2 in September 1939, when, as a result of its strategic importance, the line was closed to passenger traffic north of Lyminge and handed over to the military, which for the duration of the war continued to operate the goods service on behalf of the Southern Railway. During the early years of the war heavy rail-mounted naval guns were stationed along the line for the defence of the South Coast; these were stored on the line for protection from air attack, and in order to move them the War Department received on loan the Southern Railway's three 350hp diesel-mechanical shunters, built in 1938.

Following the end of hostilities in 1945 the line reverted to being a sleepy backwater, with passenger traffic restricted to the southern section between Folkestone and Lyminge, the remainder of the line to Canterbury being goods-only. Although the local population wanted the return of a full passenger service to prewar levels — and the Southern Railway had the intention of providing this with a new fleet of diesel railcars — this was never to be, as the line fell victim to postwar rationalisation, being closed to all traffic with effect from 16 June 1947. The line was lifted a few years later, some of the track being reused for the re-laying of the Kent & East Sussex Railway.

Over the years the Elham Valley saw a variety of motive power, including, in the early days, Cudworth '118'-class 2-4-0s and 'O' class 0-6-0s on the goods services. Later 'Q'- and 'H'-class 0-4-4 tanks operated passenger services and 'C'-class 0-6-0s on goods services, supplemented from time to time by 'N'-class 2-6-0s and even 'J'-class 0-6-4 tanks.

Carriage stock was made up of a variety of SER four- and six-wheelers and, later, non-corridor bogie stock, although Kitson steam railcars were used for a brief period before the Great War. Latterly motor trains ran on the line, with 'H'-class 0-4-4 tanks in charge.

Left: The shelter at Lyminge station *c*1928, seen from the main station building. At this time the line still had a full service. *Roger Carpenter*

Below: Picture-postcard view of Elham *c*1910, with the station platforms and signal in the foreground. *Lens of Sutton collection*

Left: The station building at Elham *c*1951, after the line had closed to all traffic. The awning had been removed as part of rationalisation in the 1930s, when the line was singled.
Lens of Sutton collection

Left: Barnham station *c*1935, after singling of the line. By this time the service had been reduced to that of a branch with a junction at each end. Goods services were now limited to a daily pick-up goods.
Lens of Sutton collection

Right: Bishopsbourne station *c*1935. The buildings on this section were not unlike those on the Hawkhurst branch, consisting of timber frames with corrugated-iron panels.
Lens of Sutton collection

Right: Bridge station *c*1935, with a few passengers waiting for the train to Canterbury East. The second line of track had been lifted after rationalisation in 1931. *Lens of Sutton collection*

THE CHATHAM CENTRAL BRANCH

The story of the Chatham Central branch is a complicated one bound up with the politics of early railway development in north Kent and the bitter rivalry between two railways and their chairmen. In 1845 the Gravesend & Rochester Railway started to run a train service along a line constructed by the Thames & Medway Canal Co from Higham to Strood through its canal tunnels and connecting at Strood with steamer services across the Medway to/from the Blue Boar and Sun piers at Rochester and Chatham respectively. In 1846 the company was acquired by the South Eastern Railway, which extended the line to Maidstone.

At this time the towns of Rochester and Chatham still had to make do with a service based on steam boats and horse-bus connections. In 1858 the London, Chatham & Dover Railway acquired the South Eastern Railway's rival, the East Kent Railway, which gave the LCDR access to Chatham and took away most of the traffic from the SER's Strood station. By 1873 the SER was planning its own line across the Medway to Chatham. However, due to a lack of finance nothing came of this, although a connecting spur had been built linking the lines of the two companies at the south end of Strood station. After much local agitation a passenger service was introduced on this spur, which had originally been used only for goods trains.

SER Chairman Sir Edward Watkin was not happy with this arrangement and was determined that his railway should build a branch of its own to Chatham, but the LCDR would not give permission for running rights over its lines for SER trains to use its station, so in 1881 the SER revived its original project of 1873 to build its own branch; by this time necessary powers had lapsed, so permission had to be obtained (in 1887) from the Admiralty and the River Medway Conservators to build the line across the river. The SER then built the branch using its own workforce, outside contractor John Cochrane & Co being responsible only for the bridge across the Medway and the brick ports. Just over a mile long, the double-track branch, which was mostly on brick viaduct, crossed the river by means of a bridge on four piers. It thus became the third fixed crossing over the Medway, the others being a road bridge and the bridge constructed by the LCDR. The SER line opened from Strood as far as Rochester Common on 20 July 1891 and was extended to Chatham Central on 1 March 1892.

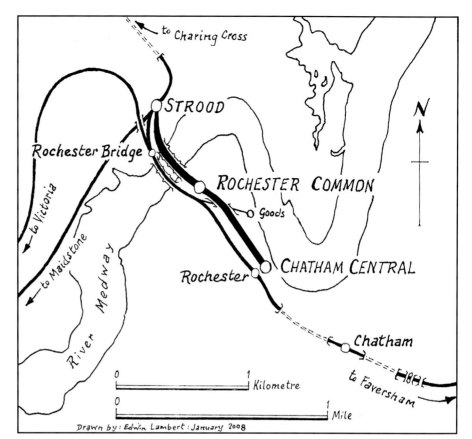

Below left: Photographs of the Chatham Central branch are very rare, as the line closed in 1911, and few photographers seem to have ventured down the line. Kitson steam railmotor No 2 stands at the station platform at Chatham Central *c*1902. *P. A. Harding collection*

Below: The only intermediate station on the branch was Rochester Common, seen being demolished *c*1912 as a 'C'-class 0-6-0 makes its way down to the goods depot. *E. Course collection*

After the formation in 1899 of the South Eastern & Chatham Joint Management Committee it was decided to rationalise lines that were loss-making as a result of duplication, and the SER branch to Chatham closed to traffic with effect from 1 October 1911. However, as part of the SECR's attempts to improve a somewhat tortuous alignment the surviving ex-LCDR main line was re-routed to use the former SER lattice-girder bridge; the LCDR bridge was subsequently demolished, and in its place now stands the present road bridge, opened in 1970.

During its existence the branch was served by a variety of locomotives including Cudworth 0-6-0 standard goods, 'P'-class 0-6-0 tanks and Kitson steam railcars. Carriage stock comprised four- and six-wheelers and, occasionally, short-wheelbase bogie stock.

THE WESTERHAM BRANCH

Whilst some of the branches covered in this volume ran through some of the bleakest and remote parts of Kent, that serving Westerham had a charm and warmth that encapsulated the county's rural railways. The people of this market town, halfway between Dunton Green and Oxted on the Kent/Surrey border, had been promised a branch line since 1864, when the South Eastern Railway had obtained Parliamentary authority for a line from Dunton Green. This was renewed in 1867 and again in 1870, but no construction work was carried out. The locals became agitated and unhappy with this situation and decided to promote and build their own line, the Westerham Valley Railway, from Dunton Green, on the South Eastern main line, to Westerham, with an extension to join up with the London, Brighton & South Coast Railway at Oxted.

The promotion of the new line made the SER sit up and take serious note. However, it was always envisaged that the line would be worked by the SER, which would also maintain the permanent way, and negotiations between the WVR's promoters and the SER duly resulted in an agreement whereby the WVR agreed to drop the scheme to build the extension to Oxted in return for co-operation from the SER.

The Act authorising the Westerham Valley Railway was passed on 22 March 1876. Sir Edward Watkin became a director, and the line's engineer, appointed by the WVR, was John William Grover;

the contractor was Charles Chamber, of Victoria Street, London. Construction work started in October 1879 and progressed swiftly, the line being opened, after a short delay due to wet weather, on 6 July 1881, when there was much celebrating, including a grand luncheon, and a free train service was provided. Regular services commenced the following day.

After opening the branch settled down to a quiet existence, trains serving the junction at Dunton Green, the intermediate station at Brasted and the terminus at Westerham, but in August 1881 the Westerham Valley Railway Co ceased to exist as a separate entity, having been taken over by the SER. In 1899 the branch became the responsibility of the South Eastern & Chatham Joint Management Committee, but otherwise things continued much as before, the only significant change being apparent from 16 April 1906, when a timber-built halt was opened at Chevening in conjunction with the introduction of the Kitson steam railmotors, which were tried at this time. Thereafter the line continued an uneventful existence until the Grouping in 1923, when it became part of the South Eastern Division of the newly formed Southern Railway.

During the inter-war period a number of changes were effected, due partly to a need for economy across the whole network. During the 1930s Chevening Halt was rebuilt using concrete components fabricated at Exmouth Concrete Works, while in 1936 a Sentinel steam railcar was tried out in an attempt to stem operating losses.

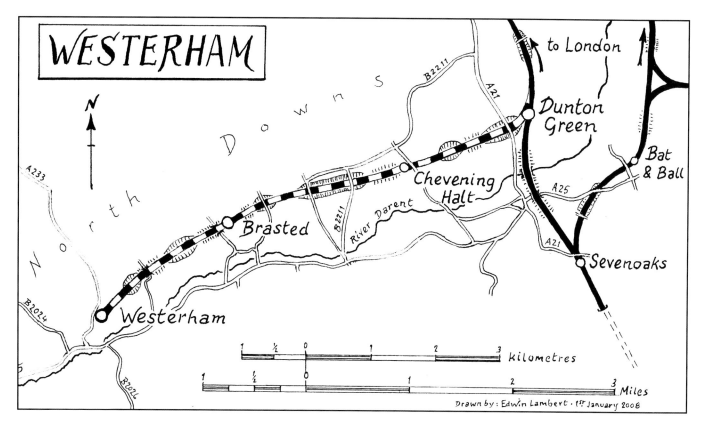

WESTERHAM

Drawn by: Edwin Lambert · 1st January 2008

These latter had been mounting since the 1920s as a result of competition from local bus and road-haulage companies, although with effect from 1 July 1933 the bus services had been taken over by the London Passenger Transport Board, which brought a certain level of stability and a co-ordination of bus and rail services at stations along the line. At this time there were some through trains between Westerham and London in the morning and evening rush hours in addition to a local service to/from Dunton Green throughout the day.

September 1939 saw the outbreak of the second great conflict of the 20th century, but, unlike most of the branches featured in this volume, the Westerham branch continued largely unaffected, surviving to become part of the newly formed British Railways' Southern Region on 1 January 1948. However, during the 1950s the need to economise became more acute, and, given that the branch had been returning operating losses for some time, it came as no surprise when, in 1961, the announcement was made that it was to close to all traffic. A concerted campaign for its retention was mounted by a supporters' group, which had been formed in the 1950s to lobby for improved services for regular commuters, and it is said that, before the final decision was made, Transport Minister Ernest Marples even travelled incognito to see the line

Left: Dunton Green in the mid-1950s, with 'H'-class 0-4-4T No 31512 and an articulated motor set awaiting the road to Westerham. The articulated sets were built from the carriage portions of ex-SECR Kitson steam railmotors. *Lens of Sutton collection*

Right: Dunton Green on 6 March 1960, this being the view down the platform towards the junction. 'H'-class 0-4-4T No 31322 waits with an articulated carriage set forming a service to Westerham. *R. K. Blencowe collection*

for himself — possibly because Sir Winston Churchill occasionally used it to travel to London from Chartwell, his country house near Westerham. However, all this was ultimately to no avail, and closure took effect on 28 October 1961. Even this need not have been the end, for a preservation society was formed to save the line and operate a commuter service to Dunton Green, but sadly this project foundered, partly because Kent County Council had decided to use part of the trackbed for construction of the M25 motorway.

During the course of its existence the line saw a variety of locomotive classes, including, in the early days, Cudworth '118'-class 2-4-0s and Stirling 'O' and 'O1' 0-6-0s. Later 'Q' and 'Q1' 0-4-4Ts were used on passenger trains, followed by 'P'-class 0-6-0Ts on motor trains and, latterly, 'H'-class 0-4-4Ts on pull-push sets. At times services were also worked by 0-4-4Ts of Classes R and R1, while 'D1', 'E1' and 'L1' 4-4-0s put in appearances on special trains. Carriage stock consisted initially of four- and six-wheelers, which were later replaced with short-wheelbase non-corridor bogie stock and pull-push motor sets.

Above: 'O1'-class 0-6-0 No 1386 simmers at the head of two ex-LBSCR bogie carriages at Dunton Green *c*1935. *Author's collection*

Left: Ex-LBSCR 'D1'-class 0-4-2T No 2355 powers a Brighton motor-carriage set nearing Chevening Halt on 3 October 1936. The 'D1' locomotives were a common sight on the Westerham line during the 1930s. *H. C. Casserley*

Right: Chevening Halt in the summer of 1960. The structure was rebuilt from a timber platform in the 1930s using concrete parts manufactured at Exmouth Concrete Works.
Lens of Sutton collection

Left: Brasted station *c*1962, shortly after closure, with snowdrifts covering the track. The station building, constructed of timber and brick, was similar in style to that at Westerham.
Lens of Sutton collection

Below: 'F'-class 4-4-0 No 458 at Westerham on 12 November 1927, having arrived from Dunton Green with a train of three ex-LCDR six-wheel carriages. This is a good example of the rolling stock used on the line at this time.
H. C. Casserley

Above: By 22 March 1936 an 'R1' 0-4-4T — No 1710 — and an articulated carriage set had replaced the rather archaic stock seen in the previous photograph. Like Brasted, Westerham had a timber-and-brick station building of SER design. *H. F. Wheeler*

Left: A quiet day at Westerham *c*1935, with 'R1' No 1700 simmering away at the head of an articulated carriage set after arriving on a service from Dunton Green. The station porter standing at the end of the platform looks rather bored. *H. C. Casserley*

Below left: A general view of Westerham station *c*1935, showing the station, goods shed with yard crane and track layout. *Roger Carpenter*

Above right: Westerham station from the opposite end of the yard shortly before closure, with the notices announcing the date of its demise already posted on the notice board (left). This photograph provides another good view of the track layout and the yard. *Lens of Sutton collection*

Right: Passengers on the platform at Westerham chat as they await the departure of 'H'-class 0-4-4T No 31184 and its train for Dunton Green on 16 July 1955. The goods shed is on the left. *R. K. Blencowe*

INDEX OF LOCATIONS ILLUSTRATED

All Hallows-on-Sea	7, 60, 61	Golgotha Tunnel	27	Richborough	33
Appledore	62, 64	Goudhurst	1, 7, 45, 46	Richborough Port	33
Barnham	103	Grain	59	Robertsbridge	8, 10, 11
Beluncle	57	Grain Crossing	59	Rochester Common	105
Biddenden	18, 19	Gravesend Central	53, 54	Rolvenden	13, 14, 15
Bishopsbourne	103	Gravesend West	98, 99	Roman Road	32
Bodiam	11, 12	Greatstone-on-Sea	67	Rosherville	97
Brambledown	37, 38	Harty Road	38	Salehurst	11
Brasted	109	Hawkhurst	6, 48, 49, 50, 51	Saltwood	92
Bridge	103	Headcorn Junction	20, 21	Sandgate	92, 93
Brookland	65	High Halden Road	18	Sandling Junction	88, 89, 90
Canterbury	74, 77	High Halstow	56	Sandwich Road	32, 33
Canterbury West	75, 76	Hoo Junction	54	Sharnal Street	56, 57
Chatham Central	104	Horsmonden	44, 45	Sheerness East	37
Chevening	108, 109	Hythe	90, 91	Shepherdswell	22, 24, 25, 26, 27
Cliffe	55	Hythe (RHDR)	70, 71	South Street	79
Cranbrook	47, 48	Junction Road	11	Southfleet	97
Dungeness	66, 67	Leysdown	39, 40	Staple & Ash	29
Dungeness (RHDR)	72	Lydd (Town)	65, 66	Stoke Junction	58
Dunton Green	106, 107, 108	Lydd Camp	66	Tenterden St Michael's	17
Dymchurch	71	Lydd-on-Sea	67	Tenterden Town	2/3, 12, 15, 16, 17
Eastchurch	38	Lyminge	100, 102	Tilmanstone Colliery	27
Eastry	28, 29	Middle Stoke	58	Tyler Hill	77, 78, 79
Eastry South	28	Minster-on-Sea	37	Uralite	54, 55
Elham	102, 103	New Romney & Littlestone-on-Sea	68, 69	Westerham	109, 110, 111
Elvington	28	New Romney (RHDR)	73	Whitstable	79, 80
Eythorne	26	Northiam	12	Whitstable Harbour	81
Farningham Road	94, 95, 96	Paddock Wood	42, 44	Wingham Canterbury Road	30, 31
Folkestone Harbour	85, 86, 87	Poison Cross	32	Wingham Town	30
Folkestone Junction	82, 83, 84	Port Victoria	59, 60	Wittersham Road	13
Frittenden Road	20	Queenborough	35, 36, 40	Woodnesborough	29